M000205495

"Lysa is one of my favorite people. It's not because she's smart or deep or caring, although she's all of these things. Lysa impresses me because she's real and transparent and honest. She's got plenty of guts and grit to get through difficult times, but what she has even more of is this—Jesus. She's learned what dazzles Him isn't our successes, but our faith. This book will point you back toward Jesus when it feels like you've lost your way."

—BOB GOFF, *New York Times* BESTSELLING AUTHOR OF *Love Does*

"Lysa has done it again! You absolutely won't be able to put down this book. It's compelling from the first page to the last. With her trademark vulnerability, Lysa lays out a heartfelt means to managing the fears, rejections, insecurities, and unsteadiness we all experience. Trust us when we tell you that you've never read a book like this before. Don't miss out. We simply can't recommend *Uninvited* enough."

—DRS. LES AND LESLIE PARROTT, #1 *New York Times* BESTSELLING AUTHORS OF *Saving Your Marriage Before It Starts*

"Lysa TerKeurst has an undeniable gift for sharing her heart's struggles in ways that strengthen and equip the lives of others. I can't remember the last time I read a book with so many insights into human nature and even more gold nuggets of biblical truth. Don't miss this book—it will bless you more each time you read it!"

—CHRIS HODGES, SENIOR PASTOR, CHURCH OF THE HIGHLANDS; AUTHOR OF *Fresh Air* AND *Four Cups*

"This book is a *must read*. Lysa speaks beautifully yet prophetically to a culture that uniquely is able to see what our friends are eating, playing, doing, and planning at any moment with the little device in our pocket. My favorite part is that Lysa turns our eyes to what's most important though, and that is the great invitation we have to sit at the table with the Living God who has been for us from the beginning."

—JEFFERSON BETHKE, BESTSELLING AUTHOR OF *Jesus>Religion* AND *It's Not What You Think*

"As a woman who has faced rejection more times than I would care to recall, *Uninvited* was the drink my thirsty soul needed. In my walk with Jesus, I have often cried out for healing and searched for words of Truth to stand on. This book has provided me with those words and also taught me so much on forgiveness. If you are searching for hope, this book has exactly what you need."

—TARA C.

"The great beauty of this book is that it doesn't just empathize with the pain of rejection, but it instills a godly courage into your soul to help you learn to walk with holy confidence. A confidence rooted in the steadfast, everlasting, wildly passionate, and abundant love of Jesus. This is a must read!"

—ALICIA S.

"Lysa's words helped me process my rejections without idolizing acceptance or neglecting the pain of them."

—MEGAN C.

"The way Lysa connects real life to Scripture helped restore my soul and helped facilitate my prayers when it seemed almost impossible to pray on my own."

—KIM C.

"This book is like a conversation between good friends that moves effortlessly from lighthearted and chatty to down and dirty, vulnerable and challenging. The danger of allowing rejection or the fear of rejection to measure our worth is at the core of many struggles women face today. Lysa confronts that issue with honesty, practicality, humor, and—most importantly—God's truth. *Uninvited* is not to be missed!"

—SARAH R.

"With the voice of a trusted friend, Lysa points the way toward a God who entered the world for the sole purpose of being rejected by His own and can understand our pain. And with the confidence of one who has taken His hand and walked through some of life's most painful valleys, she equips the reader with tools to overcome and to thrive."

—ERIN B.

"It's almost as if Lysa has seen my life and written it down. I am recommending this book to every woman I know."

—SARAH L.

"I will admit, I found myself raising my hands in tears throughout portions of *Uninvited*. Those were uniquely sweet moments with the Lord."

—EMILY S.

Uninvited

Other Books and DVD Bible Studies by Lysa

The Best Yes

The Best Yes DVD and Study Guide

Unglued

Unglued DVD and Participant's Guide

Becoming More Than a Good Bible Study Girl

Becoming More Than a Good Bible Study Girl DVD and Participant's Guide

Made to Crave

Made to Crave DVD and Participant's Guide

What Happens When Women Say Yes to God

Children's

It Will Be Okay

Win or Lose, I Love You!

Uninvited

Living Loved When You Feel
Less Than, Left Out, and Lonely

Lysa TerKeurst

NELSON
BOOKS

An Imprint of Thomas Nelson

Published in Nashville, Tennessee, by Nelson Books, an imprint of Thomas Nelson. Nelson Books and Thomas Nelson are registered trademarks of HarperCollins Christian Publishing, Inc.

Published in association with the literary agency of Fedd & Company, Inc., Post Office Box 341973, Austin, Texas 78734.

Thomas Nelson titles may be purchased in bulk for educational, business, fund-raising, or sales promotional use. For information, please e-mail SpecialMarkets@ThomasNelson.com.

Unless otherwise noted, Scripture quotations are taken from the Holy Bible, New International Version®, NIV®. Copyright © 1973, 1978, 1984, 2011 by Biblica, Inc.™ Used by permission of Zondervan. All rights reserved worldwide. www.zondervan.com. The "NIV" and "New International Version" are trademarks registered in the United States Patent and Trademark Office by Biblica, Inc.™

Scriptures marked THE MESSAGE are from *The Message*. Copyright © by Eugene H. Peterson 1993, 1994, 1995, 1996, 2000, 2001, 2002. Used by permission of Tyndale House Publishers, Inc.

Scriptures marked THE VOICE are from *The Voice*™. © 2012 by Ecclesia Bible Society. Used by permission. All rights reserved. Note: Italics in quotations from The Voice are used to "indicate words not directly tied to the dynamic translation of the original language" but that "bring out the nuance of the original, assist in completing ideas, and . . . provide readers with information that would have been obvious to the original audience" (*The Voice*, preface).

Scriptures marked ESV are from the ESV® Bible (The Holy Bible, English Standard Version®). Copyright © 2001 by Crossway, a publishing ministry of Good News Publishers. Used by permission. All rights reserved.

Scriptures marked NASB are from the New American Standard Bible®. Copyright © 1960, 1962, 1963, 1968, 1971, 1972, 1973, 1975, 1977, 1995 by The Lockman Foundation. Used by permission. (www.Lockman.org)

Scriptures marked AMPC are from the Amplified® Bible, Classic Edition. Copyright © 1954, 1958, 1962, 1964, 1965, 1987 by The Lockman Foundation. Used by permission. (www.Lockman.org)

Scriptures marked NLT are from the *Holy Bible*, New Living Translation. Copyright © 1996, 2004, 2007, 2013 by Tyndale House Foundation. Used by permission of Tyndale House Publishers, Inc., Carol Stream, Illinois 60188. All rights reserved.

Scriptures marked NLV are from the New Life Version. © Christian Literature International.

Scriptures marked KJV are the King James Version. Public domain.

Library of Congress Cataloging-in-Publication Data

Names: TerKeurst, Lysa, author.
Title: Uninvited: living loved when you feel less than, left out, and lonely / Lysa TerKeurst.
Description: Nashville: Thomas Nelson, 2016. | Includes bibliographical references.
Identifiers: LCCN 2016000389 | ISBN 9781400205875
Subjects: LCSH: Loneliness—Religious aspects—Christianity. | Rejection (Psychology)—Religious aspects—Christianity. | Christian women—Religious life.
Classification: LCC BV4911 .T465 2016 | DDC 248.8/6—dc23 LC record available at http://lccn.loc.gov/2016000389

Printed in the United States of America

16 17 18 19 20 RRD 6 5 4 3 2 1

I dedicate this book to my dearest friend Colette Greene . . . you are a gift from God and I dearly love and treasure you. I couldn't have persevered through the writing of this message without you.

And to anyone who has felt the sting of rejection, grieved the deep loss of a relationship that was there one day and gone the next, or questioned whether God has any good plans for you at all . . . I understand. God made sure to get these words of hope to you. He loves you and so do I.

Contents

I'd Rather Ignore Honesty

In the quiet of an early morning, honesty finds me. It calls to me through a crack in my soul and invites the real me to *come out, come out, wherever you are.* Not the carefully edited edition of the me I am this year. No, honesty wants to speak to the least tidy version of the woman I've become. The one I can't make look more alive with a few swipes of mascara and a little color on my lips.

Honesty is a suitor with piercing vision who isn't swayed by pretending and positioning.

I can try and make things appear better than they seem, but honesty will have none of it. So, I throw my hair in a messy bun and let my face stay splotchy. I don't suck in my stomach or whiten my teeth or spritz on some perfume.

I simply emerge.

I come out from behind all the efforts to carefully construct

1

a more acceptable version of me, and I hesitantly extend my hand, uncertain how to greet honesty. I could be met with a slap or a hug, and I'm well aware it could go either way.

I would never opt for the slap, except with me that is probably the safer of the two options. I am an incredibly awkward hugger of the worst sort. I was once introduced to a well-known pastor I was extremely nervous to meet. He was a hefty older man with a delightful soul who was determined to make me feel welcome.

I should have felt honored.

But as I saw him approaching, all the options of how to greet him danced in my brain, and I became increasingly freaked-out with every step he took toward me. I stuck out my hand. He enveloped me in a bear hug, accidentally forcing my arm down in the worst possible location. Thankfully, he quickly backed away and instead placed his hands on my shoulders to say whatever he'd planned to say.

Of course I can't tell you what he said in the end, because 243 alarm bells were going off in my head about the awkward hug possibly resulting in my being banned from every church this side of the Mississippi. Or the world.

So, since hugs aren't usually my first choice, I didn't want to hug honesty.

Actually, I've never wanted to fully embrace honesty at all. I'm much better at it today than ever before, but I hesitate, knowing just how dangerous this can be. As long as I suspect that honesty's intention is to expose me and hurt me, it will always feel like a dangerous thing.

It's easier to construct a more palatable life story—where I can draw straight lines from each hurt of the past to the healing I later experienced—than to face the raw truth. I prefer to neatly match each hard part of my testimony with the soft place I landed in the middle of God's grace, forgiveness, and restoration as proof I am walking in freedom.

Which I am. Most of the time. But honesty didn't want to talk to me about that. Honesty wanted me to bring the core of who I believe I am and hold it up to the light of what's really true.

And there's not a soul alive who will find perfect alignment there.

Not. One.

No matter how saved, sanctified, mature, and free we are, there are misalignments embedded in our souls. So this is what honesty wanted to address with me. The cause of this misalignment is something we all wish would have stayed in the middle school locker room: rejection.

One maliciously crafted rejection with my exact vulnerabilities in mind will pierce the deepest part of me. Being mature in my faith can help me better process it. It can help me have a better reaction to it. It can even help me remove the arrow and patch up the wound. But spiritual maturity doesn't shield me from rejection.

Today's rejections, big or subtle, are like stealth bombs that zing straight to my core, locating hurts from my past and making them agonizingly present all over again. They send messages that scramble up all my carefully established formulas for keeping life stable. The voices of doubt and insecurity whisper, "See, I've been telling you for years what an utter disappointment you are." Those voices don't have to scream; the pain does that in deafening tones.

So honesty stares at me, and I nod my head. I agree. There is still work to be done.

Finally, I see that honesty isn't trying to hurt me. It's trying to heal me.

———

Honesty isn't trying to hurt me.
It's trying to heal me.

———

If you want to know what's really inside a person, listen carefully to the words she speaks. Recently the Lord made sure I had an acute awareness of what some of my own words reveal. Hints of the misalignment between what's true and what I believe about myself leaked out one day at the airport. There's nothing like a serious dose of stress mixed with an extreme time crunch that makes a person's mouth forget its filter. What you really think spills out in words a little too raw and forces you to take a look at where they came from.

There I stood, staring into an empty car trunk just outside the terminal, as a stabbing realization made my heart beat fast and my thoughts swirl. I had my itinerary. I had my driver's license. I had plans to get home. But I also had a rather inconvenient realization: I didn't have my luggage. Somehow it hadn't made it into the trunk of the car.

I thought another person had grabbed it. She thought I had. So there's that.

Quickly I called a friend who was still at the hotel. I breathlessly told her of my situation and asked if she could grab my luggage and stick it on the very next shuttle headed to the airport. And one other minor detail—I only had fifteen minutes to spare before the airline would no longer allow me to check my bag.

I'm not a nail biter, so instead I nervously picked at the little threads of skin at my cuticles. I twisted my fingers until my knuckles cracked. Again, not a normal habit of mine. But this wasn't a normal moment.

Who shows up at the airport without their luggage?

I paced back and forth, willing the shuttle van to speed, but then quickly repented because my rule-following brain made me. Mentally, I was beating myself up and recounting why in heaven I hadn't made sure I had my luggage. I checked my watch. Things weren't looking good. The bus had more miles to go than I had time to wait. Ugh.

I walked over to an outside check-in counter with pleading eyes and a nervous voice, high-pitched and more than slightly annoying. "I know you don't work for the airline I'm flying, but your company is in the process of merging with it. So, is there any way I can check my luggage in here as soon as it pulls up to the curb and you can just work it all out on your computer? Please? Yes?"

"Sorry, but no," he replied. "Our computer systems aren't merged yet."

Bummer. Big huge stinking bummer.

And then I started to do what I often do when life refuses to cooperate with me. I started talking to myself. Frustration lilted and lifted from my nerves right out of my mouth. "I'm just such an idiot. I invite so much unnecessary drama and complication in my life, because my pace and my brain aren't in sync. I mean, seriously, what is wrong with my brain?!"

The luggage man made an abrupt about-face turn in my direction, extended his arm, and held up his hand, signaling me to stop. "Not in my presence," he said. "Not in my presence will you talk about yourself this way. Absolutely not."

His command startled me.

His words stopped me.

And suddenly I wondered if I was having a conversation with an angel.

"Spit happens, woman." Only he didn't say *spit*. He said, well, you know.

Great. Wouldn't you know it? I have an "angel" that cusses.

So he wasn't a divine presence, but some of his words certainly were.

They stuck to me. Like when a two-year-old spends an hour working a large lollipop into a gloopy, gummy mess and then runs her hands through your hair. That kind of sticking, it's serious.

And so was this. These words—"Not in my presence will you talk about yourself in this way"—they don't brush off easily. Nor should they. Sometimes a phrase lands in your soul with such weight it leaves the deepest impression. I collect these phrases like other people collect stamps and Beanie Babies. I fill the unlined pages of notebooks from Walmart with these phrases. These words that move me are treasures.

My fingers twitched, eager to add this to my collection, but my Walmart notebook was inside the luggage hopefully speeding, but not breaking-the-law speeding, my way. In the absence of the notebook, the only thing I could do was let the words take center stage in my mind. I heard them over and over and felt peace.

With car fumes and sharp airplane noises providing the unlikely backdrop for a church-type lesson, I realized why these words were so personally necessary for me. Negative self-talk was a rejection from my past that I had allowed to settle into the core of who I am. I talked about myself in ways

I would never let another person. Hints of self-rejection laced my thoughts and poisoned my words more than I cared to admit.

Self-rejection paves the landing strip for the rejection of others to arrive and pull on up to the gates of our hearts. Think about why it hurts so much when other people say or do things that make you feel rejected. Isn't it in part due to the fact they just voiced some vulnerability you've already berated yourself for? It hurts exponentially more when you're kicked in an already bruised shin.

Someone doesn't invite me to her event, and my thoughts recount all the faults and frailties I've voiced about myself recently. Suddenly, I assign my thoughts to that person. I hear her saying these same hurtful things. I feel labeled and judged and, yes, rejected.

Or my husband makes a comment about something I already feel sensitive about, and it incites an emotional response from me that is totally out of proportion. I find myself interpreting what he says and does way more emotionally than he ever intended. And it makes our relationship feel hard and exhausting. I feel so very rejected, and he's left scratching his head wondering why.

Or something I set my heart on unexpectedly falls through. I try to rally in my heart and remember that it's due to unforeseen circumstances. But there's some part of me that feels rejected. I don't want to take it personally, but I find myself slightly off for the rest of the day and can't quite shake the disappointment.

Or one of my adult kids makes a choice they know is the opposite of the advice I gave them. The more I push the more they pull back, and I feel like the mom I promised I'd never be: overbearing and controlling. They become quiet and distant. And I ache in deep places.

Or someone flat-out rejects me, my idea, my invitation, my kids, my project, my whatever, and it messes with me more than it should.

Relationships feel increasingly unsafe. Opportunities feel increasingly risky. And life feels increasingly uncooperative. I carry on, because that's what we girls do. But this nagging sense of rejection, real or simply perceived, is doing more of a number on me than I care to admit. Rejection steals the best of who I am by reinforcing the worst of what's been said to me.

Rejection isn't just an emotion we feel. It's a message that's sent to the core of who we are, causing us to believe lies about ourselves, others, and God. We connect an event from today to something harsh someone once said. That person's line becomes a label. The label becomes a lie. And the lie becomes a liability in how we think about ourselves and interact in every future relationship.

The line: *I don't want you* becomes the label *you aren't accepted.*

The label: *You aren't accepted* becomes the lie *you aren't worthy.*

The lie: *You aren't worthy* becomes a script of self-rejection. And it unleashes suspicion, doubt, hesitancy, and many other liabilities that hinder present relationships. We project the lines of rejection we heard from our past on others and hold them accountable for words they never said. And worst of all, we catch ourselves wondering if God secretly agrees with those who hurt us.

Rejection

steals

the *best* of

who I am

by reinforcing

the *worst* of

what's been said to me.

I would love to tell you I'm writing about this because I've overcome rejection in every way. I have made progress. I'm nowhere near as overly sensitive as I used to be. But there's a cussing "angel" who would caution me there's still work to be done.

No, I didn't choose this topic because I've mastered it. I chose this topic of rejection because I want us to dig in to the core of who we are and expose and finally heal rejection's deep infection. I'll warn you, the exposing of it all won't be tidy. But it will be honest.

And it will be good.

I can't say I'm quite ready to envelop honesty in a bear hug. I think you know the horribly awkward reason why. But I am willing to hold hands. And walk together from here.*

---

* Oh, and P.S.—I did end up making my flight. Just in the nick of time that day. I think my angel at the luggage counter was quite eager to send me on my way.

⤜⤏

Chapter 2

Three Questions We Must Consider

Several years ago we remodeled our house and tore part of the kitchen down to the studs. Since I had a vision in my mind of how I wanted things to turn out but am clueless about all things construction, I asked a very knowledgeable friend for his advice. I was so excited to get his expert opinion on fun details like where to place the appliances, cabinet colors, and lighting fixtures. But when he walked in and started staring at the ceiling with a look of grave concern, I knew something was wrong.

The beams running the length of the kitchen had been hidden by sheetrock. But now that we'd temporarily exposed them, he could see one of the major beams wasn't able to provide the necessary amount of support. About three-quarters of the way across the ceiling, the board stopped short. It wasn't long enough to extend all the way to the supporting wall. In an effort to fix it, someone had nailed into its side another board that finished extending the length of the kitchen. Not only is this not the proper way to fix a supporting beam, but the nails were barely holding things together.

But since it was just one board, I didn't understand why this was such a big deal. There were plenty of other boards doing just fine. Let's just get on with the fun decorating ideas I thought we'd be discussing.

My friend knew better.

He took me upstairs. In the exact place where the broken boards were in the ceiling below, the second floor dipped and sagged. One good jump or one heavy thing dropped in that area, and that supporting board would likely come apart.

I didn't bother to ask my friend to unpack this any further. I already knew we couldn't leave this the way it was. I walked back downstairs and stood below the problem spot.

Broken boards can't provide stability. There was nothing profound about that from a construction standpoint. Except seeing those boards barely hanging on was like looking inside myself.

For years, I'd been expecting stability from a broken identity.

When Ditches and Dads Disappoint

When I was a little girl, I had a place I'd go to hide away. We were living in a very brown apartment complex at the time. On the side of our unit near the woods and the run-down tennis court, there was a cement ditch. It was an unlikely spot for a small-framed girl who liked pink and hated bugs. From the first time I ventured down into the ditch, however, being hidden made me feel wonderfully secure.

I'm sure if I looked at it today from my adult perspective, all I'd see would be a dirty drainage ditch. But as a small girl, I loved this place where I could go out of sight from others. People passed by so unaware of me. And, though I could hear every word they were saying, I hardly paid attention. It was all just background noise.

Kids fighting over toys. Women letting gossip fly as easily as dandelion seeds. And teenage girls flirting with silly-sounding boys.

Lots of events could spin and swirl in other people's lives outside the ditch. But I remained untouched and unaffected. I was a spectator, not a participant. I loved this feeling that life could happen *around* me but not *to* me.

My world in the ditch felt predictable and therefore safe. No one ever came over to peek inside or attempt to join me. Though I'm assuming this ditch was there to carry off rainwater, that year things stayed dry. On many occasions I brought some of my treasures down to the ditch and arranged them just so, loving the feeling of being able to control my environment.

Things only changed if I changed them.

In the strangest way I felt as long as I stayed hidden, life stayed in control and I stayed safe. It was a place where scary possibilities at home couldn't touch me. But I couldn't stay in the ditch. I eventually had to go home each day. And back inside the brown apartment, things felt so very unpredictable.

I had no control of things happening around me, but they very much affected me. I now know my dad had issues and battles he was fighting that I couldn't have understood as a young girl. But at the time, I just thought he was incredibly unhappy whenever I was home. Therefore, I must be the problem.

And on some level, maybe my dad did think I was part of the problem. I complicated his life. I cost money he didn't have. And, worst of all, I was a girl.

He never wanted a girl. And I was desperate to be a treasured daughter. That's a hard equation for which there is no easy answer. My greatest fear was that my dad would one day stop coming home and I'd be no father's daughter.

In my research on rejection, I discovered two core fears that feed a person's sensitivity to rejection:

- The fear of being abandoned
- The fear of losing one's identity

As a little girl, being abandoned and losing my identity weren't words I would have used. But rejection's sting was a feeling I knew well. When a man is physically present but emotionally absent, a girl's heart can feel quite hollow and helpless. This is true whether that man is her father, her husband, or even a man whom she deeply respects.

When a man is physically present but emotionally absent, a girl's heart can feel quite hollow and helpless.

So tucked underneath my Holly Hobby blanket when the darkness of night made my heart hammer in my chest, I would whisper over and over, "God, don't let my daddy leave me. Just don't let him leave."

My dad fed my fears every day. He'd use the word *divorce* as if it were his freedom pass—not just from my mom but from me as well. He thought it no big deal to say whatever he felt. But because his words carried such weight for me, every threat of divorce was death breathing down my neck. Because if he did leave, then who would I be? A girl without a daddy felt to me like a girl without a place in this world. After all, if he couldn't love me, who would ever love me?

Love was not something that graced my dad's vocabulary. His words were harsh. But it was his silence that most terrified me. It just made me want to run to the ditch. We're all desperate to anchor our souls to something we can trust won't change. It didn't matter what the ditch looked like; it was how it made me feel safe that mattered.

But feeling safe and actually being safe are not one and the same. One day the rains came, and as the water rushed through my hiding place, it carried off all my little treasures. The ditch wasn't a safe haven. It was just a ditch, doing what ditches do. And once I saw it for what it was, I never returned. Things of this world all eventually reveal what incapable anchors they really are.

A few years later, we moved to a blue house with green carpet. And Dad stopped coming home. The last bit of what held together my security and identity splintered as he packed his things without so much as looking at me. I pressed my face against the front window and watched his car fade into a blur. And then he was gone.

Rejection settled deep into my heart. And I came to one earth-shattering conclusion: "I don't matter. I am worth nothing to my dad." And even more disturbing: "I fear I am worth nothing to God." The sum of these feelings became my new identity.

Who is Lysa?

The unwanted one.

Tearing Out the Old

After my dad left, I tried to prop up what was left of me so I wouldn't collapse into the broken place inside. Good grades. Achievements and accolades. Fun friends and good times. Boys who made me feel special. I tried to steady myself with anything that helped me feel better.

But feelings are fragile props. As are ditches that can't really hide you and daddies who won't stay.

Just like the broken beam in my house couldn't be fixed by simply nailing another board in to prop it up, neither could I. It wasn't just a better feeling that I needed; I needed a completely new way of defining my identity. I needed truth to inform what I believed about myself. Otherwise, what I believed about myself would become a fragile, flimsy, faulty foundation. The beliefs we hold should hold us up even when life feels like it's falling apart.

At that point, though, I couldn't say that the beliefs I held, held me up. For years I'd heard people talking about putting

---

The beliefs we hold should hold us up even when life feels like it's falling apart.

---

my identity in Christ. I nodded my head. I memorized by rote Colossians 3:12, which proclaimed I was one of "God's chosen people, holy and dearly loved." But when life felt threatening, I'd revert right back to the old thought patterns of feeling unloved and unwanted.

Standing underneath those broken boards helped me to see why. I couldn't keep my old broken beliefs, nail a little Jesus truth to the side, and expect stability. I knew I had to stop assessing God's goodness by how my life felt at any given time. Feelings are broken boards. Only truth is solid, unchanging, and stable through and through.

Old patterns of thought must be torn out, and a new way of looking at the core of who I am using God's truth has to be put into place. My identity must be anchored to the truth of who God is and who He is to me. Only then can I find a stability beyond what my feelings will ever allow. The closer I align my truth with His truth, the more closely I identify with God—and the more my identity really is in Him.

Here's the deal . . . when my identity is tied to circumstances I become extremely insecure because circumstances are unpredictable and ever-changing. I rise and fall with successes and failures. I feel treasured when complimented but tormented when criticized. I'm desperate to keep a relationship that makes me feel valuable. Then I'm constantly terrified of that person slipping away. Because I don't just feel like I'm losing them . . . I feel like I'm losing a big part of myself as well.

My fearful mantra is "I must keep things good so I can be good."

The exhausting manipulation and control it tak tect an identity based on circumstances will crush and hide the best of who we are behind a wall of ir

It's time to stop the lies and devastating hurt stemming from this kind of circumstantial identity. We must tie our identities to our unchanging, unflinching, unyielding, undeniably good, and unquestionably loving God. And the ties that truly bind me to Him and the truth of who I am in Him are given to me in those quiet moments where I say, "I'm Yours, God.

> I'm not who that guy says I am. I'm not who that girl says I am.
> I'm not who social media likes and comments say I am.
> I'm not who the grades, to-do lists, messes, and mess ups say I am.
> I'm not who the scale says I am or the sum total of what my flaws say I am.
> I'm going to stop flirting with the unstable things of this world so I can fall completely in love with You. I am loved. I am held. I am Yours. I am forever Yours."

The more intimacy like this that I have with God, the more secure my true identity is.

Now that we know this, the question becomes how do we live this?

Putting in the New

How do we live this out in the midst of everyday life ups and downs, acceptance and rejections, healthy days and bloated days, and all the unpredictable in-betweens? We need to develop an "intimacy-based identity," and this starts with answering three core questions:

- Is God good?
- Is God good to me?
- Do I trust God to be God?

Wrestle well with these questions using truth, and you will start to sense those new, more stable boards holding you up.

Is God Good?

I used to have a cautious approach to God. One look at the news, and one can quickly wonder, *How can a good God allow all this craziness, tragedy, and hurt?* For years, I would have answered, *What do I believe about God?* with a tilted head and a narrowed expression. "I believe He's unpredictable and slightly scary."

I didn't doubt God's power. I didn't doubt God's authority. But I did very much doubt God's goodness. However, when we go to the truth instead of our feelings for the answer to this question, we can understand God's goodness in a whole new light.

His goodness has been apparent since creation. When He formed and shaped and painted and sculpted this world and its creatures into being, His goodness seeped in with every thought and touch. "God saw all that he had made, and it was very good. And there was evening, and there was morning—the sixth day" (Genesis 1:31).

When Adam and Eve chose to sin, their sin infected and infiltrated the goodness of all God had made. So, while there are still good things in this world, the world is no longer a perfect reflection of God's goodness.

In Romans 8:21 Paul explains that the world is in "bondage to decay" or, as some versions say, in "slavery to corruption" (NASB, THE VOICE). This decay and corruption is evidence of the brokenness of this world. I personally see this evidence every time swimsuit season cycles back around. Y'all, the cellulite is real! My body is in bondage to decay. But this is a conversation for another day.

The world is in a state of decay and corruption. We see it in deadly weather patterns, natural disasters, and famines that were not part of God's good design. Cancer, sickness, and disease were not part of God's good design. Car accidents, drownings, and murders were not part of God's good design. Abuse, divorce, and relationship breakdowns were not part of God's good design.

The first sin did those things. When sin entered the world, it broke the goodness of God's design. And sin absolutely breaks God's heart. But in no way did sin affect the goodness of God. He has a plan, a good plan to rid this world of every effect of sin.

> For the Eternal is on His way:
>   *yes*, He is coming to judge the earth.
> He will set the world right by His standards,
>   and by His faithfulness, *He will examine* the people.
>
> (PSALM 96:13 THE VOICE)

Though we may get our hearts broken from the effects of sin in this in-between time, God's goodness will eventually set the world right. In the meantime, we must hold fast to the truth of who God is and His unchanging nature: God is good. His plans are good. His requirements are good. His salvation is good. His grace is good. His forgiveness is good. His restoration is good.

That is what I believe about God.

God is good.

Is God Good to Me?

Based on my experiences with my dad not wanting me, I wondered what my heavenly Father's attitude was toward me. After all, how could God just stand by and allow so much heartbreak into one little girl's world?

It seemed every three years starting the year my dad left, there was some kind of awful tragedy that cast lingering, dark shadows into my life. Abuse. Divorce. Abandonment. Mental illness. The death of my sister. A devastating breakup. The cycle just kept going and going.

Even after I'd been a Christian for a long time and knew God loved me, I still had this nagging question about why the hard stuff had to be so painful. Was God really being good to me in this? I think C. S. Lewis said it best: "We are not necessarily doubting that God will do the best for us; we are wondering how painful the best will turn out to be."[1]

And it's at this point someone at Bible study whips out Romans 8:28: "And we know that in all things God works for the good of those who love him, who have been called according to his purpose." I like that verse. And I think it helps shed some light on the reality that even if something doesn't feel good, God can still work good from it.

But verses 5 and 6 from this same chapter give me another layer of assurance:

Those who live according to the flesh have their minds
set on what the flesh desires; but those who live in
accordance with the Spirit have their minds set on what
the Spirit desires. The mind governed by the flesh is
death, but the mind governed by the Spirit is life and
peace.

What doesn't feel good in my flesh won't make sense in
my flesh. But if I have the Holy Spirit in me, my spirit is different because God is there—His indwelling presence with
me. He speaks reassurances in the spirit. He speaks comfort
in the spirit. He reminds me He is right there with me in the
spirit. Others might disappoint me and leave me . . . but God
never will.

Therefore, I have to keep my mind focused on what the
Holy Spirit whispers, not what my flesh screams.

And in my spirit I know God is good to me.

Do I Trust God to Be God?

Once we've stabilized our identity by replacing old feelings
with the solid truths that God is good and God is good to us,
now we have to answer one final question: Do I trust God to
be God?

This will not just stabilize our identities, but it will fully
anchor us. I love these verses, Isaiah 26:3–4:

> You will keep in perfect peace
>   those whose minds are steadfast,
>   because they trust in you.
> Trust in the LORD forever,
>   for the LORD, the LORD himself, is the Rock eternal.

The Hebrew word for *steadfast* used in this verse is *samak*, which means "to brace, uphold, support." Amazing, huh? In other words, those with minds fully braced, upheld, and supported by truth and trust in God will be kept in perfect peace. The mind feasts on what it focuses on. What consumes my thinking will be the making or the breaking of my identity.

Will I trust that God sees and knows things I don't? Will I trust Him when I don't understand? When circumstances are hard? When people betray or reject me? When my heart gets broken? Will I trust Him to the point where I fully turn the control of my life and those I love over to Him?

If God is good and God is good to me, then I must fill in the gaps of all the unknowns of my life with a resounding statement of trust: *God is good at being God.*

I don't have to figure my present circumstances out. I don't have to fill the silence left behind in another person's absence. I don't have to know all the whys and what-ifs. All I have to do is trust. So in quiet humility and without a personal agenda, I make the decision to let God sort it all out. I sit quietly in His presence and simply say, "God, I want Your truth to be the loudest voice in my life. Correct me. Comfort me. Come closer still. And I will trust. God, You are good at being God."

Getting Past the Past

Your story might be different from mine, but I suspect you also have past rejections that have prompted you to search for stability in various, not-always-healthy ways. The resulting hurt of any form of rejection can linger and entangle us from moving forward if we don't put it behind us. That's

The mind

feasts on

what it *focuses* on.

What consumes

my thinking will

be the *making* or

the *breaking* of my identity.

what we've been doing by ripping out those old thoughts and replacing them with a new, solid understanding of who God is and what that means for our own identities.

Remember what I said earlier in this chapter. What the mind focuses on, it feasts on. And if you want to know what a person's focus and feast is, all you have to do is listen to the words that come out of her mouth.

We live in a broken world, where rejection—even from fellow Christians—could be just around the corner. But there is good news as we wait in expectation for God's ultimate redemption! And that is Jesus. Jesus brought with Him a love that remains . . . is constant . . . stays the same.

No person's rejection can ever exempt me from God's love for me. Period. No question mark. The most beautiful love story ever written is the one you were made to live with God.

Imagine how differently you might approach each day by simply stating:

God is good.
God is good to me.
God is good at being God.
And today is yet another page in our great love story.

Nothing that happens to you today will change that or even alter it in the slightest way. Lift your hands, heart, and soul, and receive that truth as you pray this prayer:

My whole life I've searched for a love to sa *̣ ̣ ̣ ̣*
deepest longings within me to be known, tr
and wholly accepted. When You created me, L
very first thought of me made Your heart exp

a love that set You in pursuit of me. Your love for me was so great that You, the God of the whole universe, went on a personal quest to woo me, adore me, and finally grab hold of me with the whisper, "I will never let you go."

Lord, I release my grip on all the things I was holding on to, preventing me from returning Your passionate embrace. I want nothing to hold me but You. So, with breathless wonder, I give You all my faith, all my hope, and all my love.

I picture myself carrying the old, torn-out boards that inadequately propped me up and placing them in a pile. This pile contains other things I can remove from me now that my new intimacy-based identity is established.

I lay down my need to understand why things happen the way they do.

I lay down my fears about others walking away and taking their love with them.

I lay down my desire to prove my worth.

I lay down my resistance to fully trust Your thoughts, Your ways, and Your plans, Lord.

I lay down being so self-consumed in an attempt to protect myself.

I lay down my anger, unforgiveness, and stubborn ways that beg me to build walls when I sense hints of rejection.

I lay all these things down with my broken boards and ask that Your holy fire consume them until they become weightless ashes.

And as I walk away, my soul feels safe. Held. And truly free to finally be me.

Chapter 3

~

There's a Lady at the Gym Who Hates Me

There's a lady at my gym who hates me. No, I'm serious. She sees me coming, and I can feel little poofs of disdain chugging out of her ears as her feet are churning eighty-seven miles per hour on the elliptical machine. I honestly don't know how she goes so fast. I once tried to keep up with her.

It was awful.

And I think that was the day her infuriation with me began. Let me back up and confess my sins that started this whole thing. The elliptical machines are set up very close together and are completely awkward with their angular moving parts. Think if a New York high-rise and an elephant had a baby. That's an elliptical machine.

Now, conjure up a picture in your mind of the most athletic

person you know. The one who doesn't have a drop of fat on her entire body, not even at her belly button, which should be illegal in my cellulite-ridden opinion. Okay, do you have your person?

That's her. She's honestly stunningly beautiful.

Then picture a marshmallow dressed in a T-shirt and spandex pants. Her ponytail is rather tight, but not much else is. That's me. Hello, world.

So, I had to sort of get in her space just a tad to mount my machine, and I think I threw off her rhythm. That was sin number one.

And then I decided to try to stay in sync with her, because I wanted to teach all the folks at the gym that day that, though my legs and derrière might not look like it, I'm in shape. My heart can pump with the best of them. And by golly, I was tired of being out-ellipticalled by her. That was sin number two.

And then there may have been a little issue with me taking a phone call while working out. In my defense this is not at all my common practice. But a friend called who really needed me. I realize now I should have stepped off my machine and taken the call elsewhere. But I was sort of in a competition at this point and needed to win this thing on behalf of every other marshmallow-feeling woman.

I tried to chat quietly, but when you feel like a lung might very well pop out of your mouth at any minute, it's difficult to whisper-talk. That was sin number three.

Three strikes, and she deemed me out. Out of my mind. Out of line. Out of control. She abandoned her elliptical and huffed over to the treadmill. And she's hated me ever since. But then the other day, something occurred. Something odd that stunned me.

She smiled at me.

It wasn't an evil, I'm-about-to-whip-your-tail-on-the-gym-floor kind of smile. It was more like an "oh hey, I've seen you here before, right?" kind of smile. I thought about her expression the entire time on the elliptical that morning. I mean I analyzed it up one side and down the other. Was it just a stunned-reaction kind of thing, where she felt forced to smile because she couldn't quite figure out what else to do?

Or was it "I think we could be friends"?

Or was it a truce of some sort?

I've decided it wasn't any of those. I truly believe it was a simple smile acknowledging that she'd seen me but had none of this crazy hate toward me at all. It's all been a perception thing on my part. Let me rewrite the story as I now believe it actually is.

There's a lady at the gym who really enjoys her workouts. One day the gal next to her talked on the phone, so instead of making a big deal out of it, she just transitioned over to the treadmill. She really hadn't thought of it much since. And then one day she saw this same woman in the bathroom and smiled and thought, *Good for you for getting up this morning and working out.*

End of story.

Obviously, I don't know what went through her head as she smiled. But I think my second version is closer to reality than my first. Which has really gotten me thinking about all the many times I assign thoughts to others that they never actually think. I hold them accountable to harsh judgments they never make. And I own a rejection from them they never ~~

I know not every rejection is like this.

Some are completely certified and undeniable.

a just-cleaned window. And the feelings so intense they can make you as horrifically stunned as a bird soaring eastward toward the morning sun, only to slam headfirst into that clean window. The thud feels like it might just kill you. That's true rejection.

But then there's this perceived rejection, like I had with my fellow gym-goer. I don't even think I was really on her radar. But in my mind I was absolutely in her crosshairs. And so goes the crazy inside our heads sometimes.

It makes me remember something I saw an author friend of mine do several years ago that I filed away in my "Words I Love" notebook. She was signing a book. I peeked over to see what she was writing. Her approach was simple. Before signing her name she wrote, "Live loved."

Not only an instruction, but a proclamation. One that now arrests my soul and is so applicable to our discussion at hand. Live from the abundant place that you are loved, and you won't find yourself begging others for scraps of love.

How in the World Does It Really Work?

Living loved is a bit of a tricky concept. I will hand that to you along with a few more pages of my thoughts on this. Because I heard you. Just now. When you read my grand answer to "live loved" in that last section, you sighed with a big ol' "But how?"

You aren't alone.

When I posted a bit of this on my blog last year, my cyber friends were ever so clear that they liked the idea but couldn't quite connect with how this would actually work. I had typed

Live from the

abundant place

that you are *loved*,

and you won't

find yourself

begging others

for *scraps* of *love*.

up that blog and hit send with that "boo-ya" feeling you get when all of life seems solved. I did a little fist pump in the air, indicating I might just be about to party like it's 1999—in a Bible study sort of way.

"Live loved" is certainly a sermon that preaches really well. But walk outside for 2.3 seconds, and the music comes to a screeching halt while the fist pump wilts. It might preach well, but it's crazy hard to live some days. Because it's hard to live something you sometimes don't feel.

It's easy to live loved when I feel loved.

But some days I'm just not feeling it.

When life karate chops my feelings into words like *hurt*, *brushed aside*, and *left out* on Monday and then on Tuesday morning the lady at the gym smirks at me, how in heaven am I supposed to be jolly and not assume the worst? For real, it does not come naturally to me to think in those moments, *Girl, I am not picking up that negative vibe you just laid down, because I live loved.*

No way, no how.

I'm going to get into a funk, because that's what I do. I will feel put off, and then I will put on that ratty robe of rejection and wear it all day long. But I don't want to keep being a slave to my runaway emotions and assumptions. I don't want my days to be dictated by the moods of other people. And I really don't want the rejections of my past feeding my propensity to feel rejected today.

I want the kind of emotional stability I read about in the Bible:

> The LORD your God is in your midst,
>   a mighty one who will save;

> he will rejoice over you with gladness;
>> he will quiet you by his love;
> he will exult over you with loud singing.

(ZEPHANIAH 3:17 ESV)

I love the thought that God is in our midst and that He will quiet me by His love.

Yes, please. I'll take an extra-large order of that every morning. I want to believe it's possible for me not just in the middle of Bible study but in the middle of life.

So I decided to go on a "live loved" quest. I determined to be a one-woman experiment in whether or not it is actually possible to live from a place of being loved. I wanted to get to a place where my immediate reaction to off-kilter interactions with others wasn't a downward spiral of wonky feelings, but stable love instead.

It was a tall order. A venti-size order from life, really. Because immediately when I started, I struggled. My natural reaction to things happening to me was not a feeling of love.

Love is full. And I was quite empty.

I should have been happy. I knew it. I could have listed out so many things for which I was thankful. So, what was this undercurrent of disappointment that ebbed and flowed just beneath the surface of my more honest moments?

I got still, and I got sad.

Then I would see something horrific on the news that other people were facing, and I would feel so horribly guilty for even daring to give myself permission to entertain anything other than gratitude. Which just heaped shame o
sadness. I'd determine that maybe all this off-kil
just because I was running a little low on sugar a

I'd reach for a handful of something chocolate and wash it down with a Diet Coke.

Then I would rev up my Christian to-do list with all manners of serving, blessing, and giving others the kind of love I was so desperate to have boomerang back on me. Those are all good things. Fabulous activities. Biblical instructions. But when given from a heart whose real motivation is what I'm hoping I'll get in return, it's not really love at all.

That's not the answer. Giving with strings of secret expectations attached is the greatest invitation to heartbreak. That's not love. That's manipulation. And it's all so unrealistic. Only audiences are trained to applaud performances. People in everyday life can sniff out the neediness of a performer trying to earn love. Their instinct isn't to clap but rather to be repulsed by the fakeness of it all and walk away.

No soul can soar to the place of living loved when it's a performance-based endeavor. Living loved is sourced in your quiet daily surrender to the One who made you.

It's like the crazy notion I had as a little girl that ballerinas could fly. I wanted to fly. So I begged my mom for lessons and pink shoes. I wore myself out from all the leaping. Sure, I caught a bit of brief air, but never did I soar. I simply landed with a thud.

There was something crucial I misunderstood. A real ballerina doesn't attempt to fly. She simply infuses each move with such grace that the audience scarcely remembers she's as much a victim of gravity as we are. But make no mistake what you're observing when you watch her effortless elegance and softness. Underneath those floating layers of tulle perched on top of pink ribbon shoes is a soul full of disciplined grit and toes bloody from the daily practice floor.

The stage performance ending in applause isn't what enables the ballerina. It's her daily return to the instructor that, because of his love, tweaks her movements in the quiet studio. That tweaking in the quiet is the saving of her in public. And I imagine it is the instructor's approval she longs for the most. It is the source of her soaring.

We are much the same.

The gravity of living in a sin-soaked world will always try to hold us back from living loved. But if we will remember to return often to our Instructor . . . our Creator . . . we will discover His loving hands still pulse to continue making us. Tweaking us. Molding us. Filling us. And daily completing the good work He began in us.

Yes, this was what I was missing in this living-loved endeavor. I was doing many things with God in mind but not really spending time getting refilled by God and His abundant love at all. I was saying I was connecting with Him, but in all honesty, I was letting the world stir my deep affections.

I'd say, *I put God first in my life,* but give all my first moments of each day to checking my text messages rather than checking in with His message.

I'd post a Bible verse and return fifteen times that next hour to see how many likes I got.

I'd think, *I am doing everything I can to protect my marriage,* but then watch a movie with so much airbrushed love that I couldn't help but be slightly disappointed with my reality.

I'd believe I had prayed about things, but in reality I'd only worried about them, talked to friends about them and tried to figure out how to solve them myself.

How dangerous it is when our souls are gasping

we're too distracted flirting with the world to notice. Flirting will give you brief surges of fun feelings but will never really pull you in and hold you close. Indeed, the world entices your flesh but never embraces your soul. All the while, the only love caring enough to embrace us and complete enough to fill us, waits.

He waits every day with every answer we need, every comfort we crave, every affection we're desperate for, while we look everywhere else but at Him.

I was quite simply getting it wrong. Maybe you can relate? We run at a breakneck pace to try and achieve what God simply wants us to slow down enough to receive. He really does have it all worked out. The gaps are filled. The heartache is eased. The provision is ready. The needs are met. The questions are answered. The problems are solved.

We run at a breakneck pace to try and achieve what God simply wants us to slow down enough to receive.

Fully.
Completely.
Perfectly.
In Him. With Him. By Him.
We just have to turn to Him. And sit with Him. No matter what. Even if our toes are bloody from the constant wear and tear of desperately running to Him. Get to Him daily.

How it must break His heart when we walk around so desperate for a love He waits to give us each and every day.

Imagine a little girl running with a cup in her hand sloshing out all it contains. She thinks what will refill her is just ahead. Just a little farther. She presses on with sheer determination and clenched teeth and an empty cup clutched tight.

She keeps running toward an agenda He never set and one that will never satisfy. She sees Him and holds out her cup. But she catches only a few drops as she runs by Him, because she didn't stop long enough to be filled up. Empty can't be tempered with mere drops.

The tragic truth is what will fill her—what will fill us—isn't the accomplishment or the next relationship just ahead. That shiny thing is actually a vacuum that sucks us in and sucks us dry . . . but never has the ability to refill. I should know, because that's where I was. There's no kind of empty quite like this empty: where your hands are full but inside you're nothing but an exhausted shell.

Since my fast-paced chase had gotten me into this mess, I knew it would take slow moments to get me out of it. I needed to reconnect with the One who knows how to breathe life and love back into depleted and dead places. Jesus doesn't participate in the rat race. He's into the slower rhythms of life, like *abiding, delighting,* and *dwelling*—all words that require us to trust Him with our place and our pace. Words used to describe us being with Him.

"If you abide in Me, and My words abide in you, ask whatever you wish, and it will be done for you." (JOHN 15:7 NASB)

Delight yourself in the LORD,
    and he will give you the desires of your
                                    (PSA1

Jesus doesn't participate

in the rat race.

He's into the slower rhythms

of life, like *abiding,*

delighting,

and *dwelling* —

all words that require us

to trust Him with our place

and our pace.

He who dwells in the secret place of the Most High shall
remain stable and fixed under the shadow of the Almighty
[Whose power no foe can withstand]. (Psalm 91:1 AMPC)

Did you catch the beautiful filling promised in each of
those verses? When we abide, delight, and dwell in Him, He
then places within us desires that line up with His best desire
for us. Therefore, He can give us whatever we ask, because
we will only want what's consistent with His best. He can
fully satisfy our hearts, because they are consistent with His
heart. He can promise us stability, because we're tapped into
His consistent power.

This is the fullness of the person who can truly live loved.

This was the kind of fullness I needed to properly process
the woman at the gym. This is the kind of fullness I need in
every situation I face. And it's certainly the kind of fullness
I'll need as I continue to live out the calling on my life to bring
the love of Jesus to this desperate world.

As a matter of fact, when Jesus appointed the disciples
(Mark 3:14–15), there were two parts to their calling: "He
appointed twelve that they *might be with him* and that he
might *send them out to preach and to have authority to drive
out demons*" (emphasis added). Yes, they were to go out to
preach and drive out demons, but the first part of their calling was *to be with Him.*

Fullness comes to us when we remember to be with Him
before going out to serve Him. He wants our hearts to be in
alignment *with* Him before our hands set about doing today's
assignment *for* Him.

So, He extends what we need and invites us each day to
receive in prayer, worship, and truth from His Word. And He

lovingly replenishes our cups while whispering, "This isn't a race to test the fastest pace. I just want you to persevere on the path I have marked out especially for you. Fix your eyes not on a worldly prize but on staying in love with Me."

Then, and only then, will I stop flirting with this world. And, instead, operate from the full assurance of His love.

It's not deciding in my mind, *I deserve to be loved.* Or manipulating my heart to feel loved. It's settling in my soul, *I was created by God, who formed me because He so much loved the very thought of me. When I was nothing, He saw something and declared it good. Very good. And very loved.*

Therefore, I can bring the atmosphere of love into every situation I face. I don't have to wait for it, hope for it, or try to earn it. I simply bring the love I want. Then I'm not so tempted to flirt with the world, hoping for approval, because I have the real thing with God. And I'm not nearly as likely to fall into perceiving rejection that isn't really there, because I'm not starving for affection.

I am loved. This should be the genesis thought of every day. Not because of how terrific I am. God doesn't base His thoughts toward me on my own fragile efforts.

No, God's love isn't based on me.

It's simply placed on me. And it's the place from which I should live . . . loved.

God's love isn't based on me. It's simply placed on me. And it's the place from which I should live . . . loved.

Chapter 4

≈

Alone in a Crowded Room

I wished the small room would open up and swallow me whole. Just envelop me into an abyss that would simultaneously hide me and remove me. It's painful to be in a crowded room and feel all alone. Everyone had someone. Their chatting and laughing lilted and lifted in a symphony of connection. I looked around, and there wasn't a soul I recognized. Fifty-plus strangers to me but apparently friends with one another.

My brain demanded I just walk up and introduce myself to someone—anyone. But my heart sensed they were all knee-deep in conversations that would be super awkward for me to break into. Desperate for my aloneness not to become painfully obvious to others, I knew I had to look busy. And intentional. And effortlessly okay with my solo status.

I whipped out my phone with such urgency it would seem

the world might just stop on a dime if I didn't attend to some urgent matter. I refreshed my Instagram four times. And I answered an e-mail. It was crucial to thank my vet at that very moment for the reminder of my dog needing shots. Good gracious, what had my world come to?

I felt like glances of pity were stabbing me. Hello, middle school. I thought I had rid myself of you when I was but a wee, tiny thing with no such words as *cellulite* and *stretch marks* in my vocabulary. But obviously not.

Time to move across the room. *Please, Lord, let me get the vibe from someone, anyone, that it would be okay for me to join in their conversation.* I walked over to the food table. Three carrot sticks and four stalks of broccoli with some ranch never looked so appealing since it gave me something to do. Something other than count the dots on the swirls of the patterned carpet.

And then I spotted what I hoped to be my saving grace. The dude serving soda! He was standing behind a table full of water bottles and cans, looking utterly fascinated with absolutely nothing. Score. He could be my person for at least ten minutes if I could think of enough questions to ask him.

Surely I would remind him of his mom or sister or his cousin whom he had to take to prom last year to appease his begging aunt. And he would be so happy to fill the conversational needs of this desperate, frizzy-haired girl. Which, of course, would give me something else to chat with him about: hair situations. Yes!

Beyond brilliant.

I could explain to him that my hair frizzes when I sweat, unless I use this amazing product that I pay my hairdresser too much for but I'd forgotten to pack for this trip and so . . .

ha-ha . . . it looks like I'll get a call from the '80s any minute, asking for their hairstyle back. Then we'd both laugh, and this young soda boy would suddenly become my BFF for the rest of this painful gathering.

For real. This was a good plan.

So, with great expectations I walked up and decided to just play it cool with my first question. Then I'd get to the hair frizz and the '80s calling and him being my new BFF. But first things first. After all, I didn't want to appear desperate, you know?

So, I asked where he was from. Best first question ever. Except when he replied, "Here," and then turned and walked back to the kitchen. I wanted a do-over. I should have jumped right into the whole hair talk! At least that would have held him hostage for at least five minutes. Now I had nothing. Except the desire to chase him into the kitchen and ask if I might hide in the pantry for the next hour or so.

I endured ten more minutes of nothingness at this gathering and then made up an excuse to tell the host why I needed to scoot. Note the carefully chosen word *scoot*. Which was code for hustle as quickly as possible back to my hotel room, dive into the lumpy bed, and pull the covers over my head for days or possibly forever. That was yet to be determined.

Isn't it strange how you can literally rub shoulders with lots of people but feel utterly alone? Proximity and activity don't always equal connectivity.

---

*Proximity and activity don't
always equal connectivity.*

On the surface, connectivity seems to require that I connect with other people and they connect back with me. Of course that gathering I was at was an extreme example of being alone in a crowded room, but that feeling isn't sequestered to that one incident. I can get it when things grow cold and too quiet with my husband. And deep down inside of me, I want to ask for forgiveness, but my pride is holding all my kind words hostage. So the silent treatment continues. And though he's right there beside me, we're nowhere near connecting.

And that feeling can happen when I'm with a group of women, and I can't quite seem to break into the conversation. I mentally beat myself up for not being more brilliant or caught up on the world's current events and fashion trends. They all seem so effortlessly on top of everything. They are even able to only eat six bites of a no-carb lunch and be completely satisfied. I order a water with lemon instead of a Diet Coke and feel like it's a major diet victory. I sit back as an observer and end my attempts at connecting by eating three more slices of bread.

Or I'm at a conference with fellow writers, and everyone else's ideas sound a million times more creative and cutting-edge than mine. So, I slip my contribution into my bag and stay quiet. My hope to brainstorm and share collective insights withers into a few nods and oohs and ahs manufactured from that manners class my mom made me take. I encourage, but I don't connect.

In each of these situations I'm with people. But I'm so very alone.

And I secretly ponder how the events of that day clearly point out other people's issues: their self-focus, their past problems, their insensitivity. Blah, blah, don't you want a little invitation to my pity party? While I think I'm seeing with crystal clarity that the problem is everyone else, I'm blinded by the very same things I deem them guilty of demonstrating.

Yes, there was a problem.

But the problem wasn't the people at the party. The problem wasn't my husband or that group of women or those fellow writers. It was me not being prepared in advance with a fullness that can only come from God.

It was as if I walked into each of these situations suddenly feeling like I wouldn't be able to breathe unless someone else invited me in. The whole room was full of completely breathable air, but since I refused to take it in, I suffered.

I can't expect any other person to be my soul oxygen. I can't live as if my next breath depends on whether or not they give me enough air for my lungs not to be screaming in pain. Because here's the thing. People don't mind doing CPR on a crisis victim, but no person is equipped to be the constant lifeline to another.

We must respect ourselves enough to break the pattern of placing unrealistic expectations on others. After all, people will not respect us more than we respect ourselves.

No, it's not wrong to need people. But some of our biggest disappointments in life are the result of expectations we have of others that they can't ever possibly meet. That's when the desire to connect becomes an unrealistic need. Unrealistic neediness is actually greediness in disguise. It's saying, "My needs and desires deserve to tap into or possibly even deplete yours." This will never set a relationship up for success.

Here's the secret shift we must make: Do I walk into situations prepared with the fullness of God in me, free to look for ways to bless others?

Or . . .

Do I walk into situations empty and dependent on others to look for ways to bless me?

People prepared with the fullness of God in them are not superpeople with pixie dust sparkles of confidence oozing from the pores from which normal people simply sweat. They aren't the ones who walk into a room with the boisterous, "Hey, hey, hey! The party can start now, because I have arrived!" And they certainly aren't the ones who circle the room, making sure their agenda is *the agenda* of every conversation.

No, the fullness of God is tucked into the sacred places within them. The full taking in of God is their soul oxygen. It's not that they don't need people. They do. God created them for community. But the way they love is from a full place, not from an empty desperation. As we talked about in the last chapter, they are living loved.

But living loved isn't just their mind-set; it is a choice they make daily. It isn't just a possible thing they should try. It's the only solution that actually works. We have to tell our minds to live loved. But then we must also tell our flesh no.

The more we fill ourselves from His life-giving love, the less we will be dictated by the grabby-ness of the flesh.

I want this. And I suspect you do too.

Being full of God's love settles, empowers, and brings out the best of who we are. On the other hand, the more full of the flesh we are, the more we grab at anyone and anything to fill that ache for love and acceptance.

I don't like to ache. In any way. One of my aches is from my deep Italian fondness for anything pasta. I mean for real, I love pasta, but it does not love me back. So, I have to make the choice not to risk the temporary pleasure of my taste buds for what will surely be hours of rebellion in my stomach. My flesh begs me to believe that short-term happiness is worth the long-term misery.

But I've discovered something about defeating the flesh. If I fill my stomach with healthy foods before being tempted with the pasta, I can say no. It's so much easier to turn away a dish of pasta if you're completely full already. But if you are desperately hungry, a dish of just about anything is hard to turn away. Our souls and our stomachs are alike in this way.

One of the most beautiful descriptions of the fullness of God is found in Paul's prayer for the Ephesians:

> For this reason I kneel before the Father, from whom every family in heaven and on earth derives its name. I pray that out of his glorious riches he may strengthen you with power through his Spirit in your inner being, so that Christ may dwell in your hearts through faith. And I pray that you, being rooted and established in love, may have power, together with all the Lord's holy people, to grasp how wide and long and high and deep is the love of Christ, and to know this love that surpasses knowledge— that you may be filled to the measure of all the fullness of God. (Ephesians 3:14–19)

My favorite part of Paul's prayer is him asking that we have the power to *grasp* the fullness of the love of Christ . . . for then we will *be filled* with the fullness of God. It is impossible to grasp the fullness of God without grasping the fullness of the love of Christ.

At the core of who we are, we crave the acceptance that

comes from being loved. To satisfy this longing we will either be graspers of God's love or grabbers for people's love.

If we grasp the full love of Christ, we won't grab at other things to fill us. Or if we do, we'll sense it. We'll feel a prick in our spirit when our flesh makes frenzied swipes at happiness, compromising clutches for attention, paranoid assumptions with no facts, joyless attempts to one-up another, and small-minded statements of pride. We'll sense these things, and we'll be disgusted enough to at least pause.

In this pause lies the greatest daily choice we can make. Am I willing to tell my flesh no, so that I can say yes to the fullness of God in this situation? Here's where I get in trouble. And here's where I got in trouble that day at the party. And here's where I bet you get tripped up as well.

I grasp the love of Christ.

I sense when I'm making choices that don't reflect God's love.

I'm disgusted by those choices.

I am willing to tell my flesh no.

I'm just not sure *how* to tell my flesh no.

When past rejections make me so prone to satisfying or at least numbing the flesh to avoid more pain, it's hard to resist.

When you're lonely and you see your ex-boyfriend post a picture with a new girl, laughing, holding hands, and looking like the happiest they've ever been, your flesh will want to grab at something. It's hard not to comfort yourself by texting another guy to grab a little attention and make yourself feel better.

When you're listening to other moms talking about all the progress their children are making in reading and your child can't even identify letters yet, your flesh will want to grab at something. It's hard not to throw out a statement to one-up the bragging moms in an area where your child is excelling.

When your husband isn't answering his cell so you call his workplace only to learn he left early for the day, your flesh will want to grab at something. Paranoia seizes you, and by the time he walks in the door you all but accuse him of having an affair.

All these things we're tempted to grab at? They won't fill us the way we think they will. In the end, they only make us feel emptier and more rejected.

Yes, the concept of telling our flesh no can sound so good on paper, but in the midst of rejection's painful pricks, we can often feel so very powerless. That's where we have to know we aren't expected to just put on a brave face and hope for the best. We have the power through Christ, who is over every power, including the pull of the flesh and the sting of rejection. When we have Christ, we are full—fully loved and accepted and empowered to say no.

This is true on the days we feel it and still true when we don't feel Jesus' love at all. If we live rooted and established in His love, we don't just have knowledge of His love in our minds, but it becomes a reality that anchors us. Though winds of hurt and rejection blow, they cannot uproot us and rip us apart. His love holds us. His love grounds us. His love is a glorious weight preventing the harsh words and hurtful situations from being a destructive force. We feel the wind but aren't destroyed by it. This is the "fullness of God" mentioned in the verses from Ephesians 3 that we just read.

There is power in really knowing this. This isn't dependent on what you've accomplished. Or on another person loving you or accepting you. Nor is it because you always feel full. You are full, because Christ brought the fullness to you.

Yes, I am fully loved, fully accepted, and fully empowered to say no to my flesh. Speak that truth in the power He's given you. Believe that truth in the power He's given you. Live that truth in the power He's given you.

That's how you tell your flesh no. That's how you live fully prepared in the fullness of God.

In the Fullness of God

When I walked into that gathering, I could have been fully prepared by saying to myself, "I bring the fullness of God into this room with me. Therefore, I am on assignment to bring His acceptance and love into this place."

This isn't some legalistic attempt to earn points with God. This is an authentic way to live as someone who knows she is truly loved by God. I really appreciate Eugene Peterson's take on Galatians 5:22–25, which seems to sum up living out the fullness of God in the everyday details of our lives:

> But what happens when we live God's way? He brings gifts into our lives, much the same way that fruit appears in an orchard—things like affection for others, exuberance about life, serenity. We develop a willingness to stick with things, a sense of compassion in the heart, and a conviction that a basic holiness permeates things and people. We find ourselves involved in loyal commitments, not needing to force our way in life, able to marshal and direct our energies wisely.

Legalism is helpless in bringing this about; it only gets in the way. Among those who belong to Christ, everything connected with getting our own way and mindlessly responding to what everyone else calls necessities is killed off for good—crucified.

Since this is the kind of life we have chosen, the life of the Spirit, let us make sure that we do not just hold it as an idea in our heads or a sentiment in our hearts, but work out its implications in every detail of our lives. (THE MESSAGE)

It's time we prepare ourselves, right now, with the fullness of God. Before that next party. Before that next difficult discussion with our husbands or friends or neighbors. Before that next step we take in pursuing our dreams. Before that next hurt, hurdle, or heartbreak. We must get this settled in our hearts, minds, and souls.

In light of God's deep affection, we no longer have to live in fear of rejection.

The more fully we invite God in, the less we will feel uninvited by others.

The more fully

we *invite* God in,

the less we will feel

uninvited

by others.

Chapter 5

Hello, My Name Is Trust Issues

I have lived entirely too much of my life hesitant. I'm a pon-derer, an analyzer, a girl who rearranges thoughts and things to be more orderly. I'd like for all life's events to line up with quite a bit of predictability so that I can sense my people and I are headed in the general direction of joy and peace.

I crave for life to make sense.

I cringe when it doesn't.

So, I wrestle through my questions in prayer. I say wrestle because I'm forever making suggestions and predictions. It's as if I'm saying to God, "Here's the plan, and, trust me: it's really good, God. So, if you could bless all this . . . don't mess with all this . . . just bless it and we'll be good."

As. If. I. Have. Any. Clue.

Hello, my name is Trust Issues. It's nice to meet you.

I want life to be as stable as a math problem. Two plus two

always equals four. It will equal four today. It will equal four tomorrow. And it will equal four into the tomorrows years from now.

Math equations don't experience breakups and letdowns. They don't get cancer. Or have their best friend get transferred and move across the country. They don't have affairs or unmatched affections. They are highly predictable. Therefore, they are easy to trust.

Life and relationships aren't nearly as tidy. They are more like loose threads. Sometimes you pull at a loose thread, and it snaps off just as you thought. Perfect. Problem solved. But then another day you try this with a different outfit, and when you pull, the whole garment unravels layer by layer. You're left with a heap of tangled threads you can't possibly weave back together.

It doesn't make sense. You didn't see this coming. You weren't prepared for the outcome. We stare at and cry over this unexpected loss. And it makes us ever so hesitant to pull another thread or try a new relationship. They both feel incredibly and impossibly risky in a world so full, too full, of the unexpected.

Especially when rejection was the cause of some of your unexpected losses, the hesitant girl can easily become flat-out resistant. And if we aren't careful, being resistant can easily turn into being rebellious against divine opportunities.

Life doesn't add up. People don't add up. And in the rawest moments of honest hurting, God doesn't add up. All of which makes us hold our trust ever so close to our chests until it becomes more tied to our fears than to our faith. That's where I was when Bob and Maria stuck out their hands to shake mine and invite me to their mountain home. I knew of them.

We run in the same circles. Do life with some of the same people. Like the same kinds of things.

But I didn't know them, know them. And because I'd had a little string of unfortunate situations, I was—how does that rock song put it—"once bitten twice shy." Only I was more like ten times bitten a hundred times shy. And resistant. And teetering on the edge of being rebellious. I didn't want to open up myself to yet another possible complicated disappointment.

I reasoned, *Walk away early so you don't have to suffer the pain of them falling away later.* Some call that protecting yourself. But I knew in my case it was called letting past hurts hurt me all over again.

I graciously told them they were incredibly kind to offer and I would absolutely check to see if this could work . . . but I really didn't think it would. And while I was saying this with expressions of possibility on my face, I knew there was zero possibility in my heart.

No way. No how.

They were having a retreat at their mountain home with an eclectic group of some of their favorite people, and somehow I got on that list. On the one hand, I was so honored that they had thought of me. On the other hand, I was slightly freaked-out that they had thought of me.

So, I absolutely knew I wasn't going. Except at the last minute I typed yes and accepted their invite. I have no idea how that happened.

I trekked literally by plane, bus, and boat to a place so tucked away and untouched by everyday realities that not even the Internet had ever been there. Or a cell tower.

This was either going to be a truly amazing getaway or one after which my people would never see me again and I'd be featured on some *Dateline* show where Keith Morrison's deep and mysterious voice would say, "It all started with a strange invitation to a strange place with strangers who turned into dangers."

My brain is so very prone to run off to the worst-case scenarios and start writing ominous news stories about tragedies that never happen. For. Real.

But the minute we pulled up to the peaceful mountains diving straight down into a lake so clear it mirrored the sky's every detail, I knew I would be just fine. God had obviously kissed this place. And it was at this place where God would untangle some of my trust issues.

The first day came and went without me wishing I could sprout wings and fly home. The only time I came close was when I got picked to be on the synchronized swimming team. And due to a little scheduling snafu, there was no time to (ahem) shave before donning a bathing suit in front of the entire group. So, I improvised by wearing long spandex pants and a T-shirt.

This was fine until one well-meaning dude asked if I was part of a religious order that forbade women from wearing bathing suits. Since I believe honesty is the very best policy, I simply said, "No, dude. I just didn't want the hair on my legs to stab the people getting close to me. And then there's this deal I have with cellulite, so basically these pants were sort of a win-win for all involved."

The expression on his face told me he'd be telling stories about me for days. Other than that—and the other small fact that my assigned roommate was a teen television star who my people *adore* and would die a thousand deaths if they knew I was now practically her BFF—things stayed casual the first day.

(And by BFF I mean I basically admitted to her I sometimes

snore and gave her total permission to punch me if said occurrence woke her up at night. And then I slept sitting up, so afraid I would also give her stories for days. So, yeah, we bonded.)

After surviving day one, I went into day two a little more confident. Big mistake. You know you are in trouble when they hand you a helmet to put on before the next activity. The ropes course.

I'm sure you have discerned I'm not the most athletic person. Or daring. Or fond of unpredictable outcomes, especially when my brain is screaming, "Death is but one slip away!" So, putting me up in the trees with nothing but ropes to stabilize and stop me from falling? Not the best of situations. I bossed my heart to stay in my chest and my lungs to remember to keep taking in air. I shook and shimmied and stammered all the way through to the very last station.

That's when I realized the grand dismount of this course was a leap from a platform to catch a bar suspended several feet away. You might as well have told me to jump from North Carolina to California and, right about the time I'm passing the Grand Canyon, to grab hold of a toothpick in midair. Every bit of saliva disappeared from my mouth, making it impossible to properly express to the ropes-course workers it was time for me to locate the emergency exit.

Because there was no way on God's green earth they were going to get me to jump.

And then Bob appeared. With his enormous smile, grandfather-gray hair, and arms magnetic with the purest grace, he drew me over to the edge.

"Lysa, this isn't about finishing the ropes course. This is about conquering your hesitancy, resistance, and fear. These ropes holding you will only let you slightly drop if you miss the bar. Then they will catch, and you absolutely will not fall," he whispered as if he had a window view inside of my soul.

I looked at the space between the edge of the platform and the bar. I saw death. Bob saw life.

What a visual for the word *trust.*

What we see will violate what we know unless what we know dictates what we see.

Bob knew the ropes would hold me. Therefore, he looked at the gap of the unknown with the full assurance that my jump would be good. Life-giving. Thrilling to capture the abstract word of *trust* and turn it into an event so concrete I'd never forget it. The word *trust* is like air; you know it's there but it's tough to draw a picture of it. Bob knew this jump had the potential to be an absolute masterpiece that would hang in my mind's gallery of faith.

But, best of all, Bob knew that my ability to survive this jump had absolutely nothing to do with my efforts. I was held safe standing on the platform. I would be held safe in midair. And I would absolutely be held safe whether or not I caught the bar.

My safety was not dependent on my performance.

I felt the exact opposite of Bob.

No matter what Bob said, I felt my very life depended on whether or not I was capable of catching the bar. Since I felt weak, the jump felt impossible. Whether I lived or died was all dependent on my performance.

And worst of all, I did not feel held safe. Girls who have the lingering whispers of rejection still echoing in the hollows of their soul rarely feel completely held safe. So they look at gaps of the unknown and hesitate at best. Run away at worst. They crave for life to make sense. They cringe when it doesn't. It's

What we see

will *violate* what

we *know* unless

what we know

dictates what

we *see*.

unfathomable to take a leap into something as uncertain as air and expect to stay intact.

Trust for me was a word to use in giving an answer at Bible study or to sing in a praise song. Good in theory but bad in practicality. To use it in real life was complete and utter foolishness that would lead to brokenness. Or, in this case, death.

"Jump, Lysa," Bob urged.

"I can't," I squeaked. "Even if I want to, I can't figure out how." My feet and my brain had become disconnected. The signals weren't reaching the fibers of my muscles. I couldn't jump. Neither could I turn and run. By this point an audience was gathering below. They started chanting my name and cheering for me to jump.

I felt utterly exposed.

Bob whispered, "You are absolutely loved. Now, when you're ready, jump."

I can't tell you how long I stood there. It felt like days and milliseconds all at the same time. The world swirled and tilted and shifted without me so much as twitching a muscle fiber. I forgot to breathe. I couldn't even blink.

David Trembled Too

I would imagine you've been in situations that have felt quite paralyzing as well.

David from the Bible certainly knew this feeling.

And one of the most popular of David's writings is perfect for times like these. Now, even if you've read this psalm many times before, don't skip this. I have something so sweet to show you.

I don't know when David wrote Psalm 23. But I do know at

some point in his life David learned how to tremble well at the crossroads of trust. Though there were certainly times he waffled, I see him over and over leaping toward God.

> The LORD is my shepherd, I lack nothing.
> > He makes me lie down in green pastures,
> he leads me beside quiet waters,
> > he refreshes my soul.
> He guides me along the right paths
> > for his name's sake.
> Even though I walk
> > through the darkest valley,
> I will fear no evil,
> > for you are with me;
> your rod and your staff,
> > they comfort me.

> You prepare a table before me
> > in the presence of my enemies.
> You anoint my head with oil;
> > my cup overflows.
> Surely your goodness and love will follow me
> > all the days of my life,
> and I will dwell in the house of the LORD
> > forever.

David started this stunning soul declaration with the assurance that with God there is fullness. There is no lack. Nothing can be added or subtracted with human acceptance or rejection. With the fullness of God, we are free to let humans be humans—fickle and fragile and forgetful.

With the fullness of God, we are
free to let humans be humans—
fickle and fragile and forgetful.

The Bible reminds us of this many times:

- What, then, shall we say in response to these things? If God is for us, who can be against us? (Romans 8:31)
- For God has said, "I will never fail you. I will never abandon you." So we can say with confidence, "The LORD is my helper, so I will have no fear. What can mere people do to me?" (Hebrews 13:5–6 NLT)
- The LORD is my light and my salvation—whom shall I fear? The LORD is the stronghold of my life—of whom shall I be afraid? (Psalm 27:1)

The peace of our souls does not rise and fall with unpredictable people or situations. Our feelings will shift, of course. People do affect us. But the peace of our souls is tethered to all that God is. And though we can't predict His specific plans, the fact that God will work everything together for good is a completely predictable promise.

Just like those ropes wrapped around and around my body holding me to the course from beginning to end, these verses wrap our souls with steady assurance. God will lead us, comfort us, guide us, walk with us, prepare the best for us, and continue filling us with such lavishness that we're not just full but overflowing.

All of this is certain. No more need for hesitancy. But here's the one thing we must watch out for: If we become enamored with something in this world we think offers better fullness than God, we will make room for it. We leak out His fullness to make room for something else we want to chase.

It will happen if you chase a guy you think will make you
   more full.
It will happen if you chase an opportunity you think will
   make you more full.
It will happen if you chase some possession you think will
   make you more full.
It will happen if you, like me, chase perfect order from an
   imperfect world, thinking it will make you more full.

But at some point every one of those things will reveal its absolute inability to keep us full. And then, since we denied God's power to lead us, we forget His power to hold us. In an effort not to free-fall, we chase something or someone else we think will ease our emptiness.

David takes a different approach. He reminds himself at the end of this psalm of trust and fulfillment:

> Surely your goodness and love will follow me
>   all the days of my life,
> and I will dwell in the house of the LORD
>   forever.

> (PSALM 23:6)

There is a certainty in what David is declaring here. It's not based on a feeling or a good circumstance. It's based on what David knows to be unchanging truth. There aren't many sure things in this world. But God's love and goodness are something we can absolutely count on to be there with us . . . to *follow* us.

That word *follow* in the original Hebrew is *radaph*, meaning "to pursue" or "chase." God's goodness and love will run after us all the days of our lives. How tragic that when we chase something in this world, we're actually running away from the stable trust and secure love our souls long for the most. Our souls were created to be pursued and fulfilled by God's love and goodness. Other chases deplete us and erode our trust.

On the platform that day in the woods, my soul was forced to be still. And as I got still, the Lord's pursuit of me became increasingly clear.

Bob whispered one final thing: "It's already done."

I don't know exactly what he meant, but I know what my soul heard. *God has already caught me. His goodness and love have pursued me and won me. I just need to jump into that reality.* And without any other conscious thought, my soul kicked in where my brain could not. My feet exploded off the platform and into midair.

I touched the bar, but I did not catch it.

I didn't need to.

Because trust caught me.

One of the last things we did before this weekend ended was a ceremony where Bob sat with each of us individually. When it was my turn, Bob took a piece of boat rope and placed it around my wrist. He carefully burned the ends and pressed them together. It formed a bond in more ways than one.

It's a bracelet. It's a reminder. It's a touchable link to the day I found trust in midair.

Pray with me:

Lord, You are teaching me so much about trusting You. Fully. Completely. Without suggestions or projections I'm choosing to embrace the very next thing You show me. I'll take this first step. And then I'll take the next.

I finally understand I don't have to fully understand each thing that happens for me to trust You. I don't have to try and figure it out, control it, or even like it, for that matter. In the midst of uncertainties, I will just stand and say, "I trust You, Lord."

I visualize me taking my fear of rejection from my incapable clutches and placing my trust in Your full capability. And as I do, I make this all less about me and more about You. I replace my fragile efforts to control with Your fortified realities.

You are the perfect match for my every need.

I am weak. You are strength.

I am unable. You are capability.

I am hesitant. You are assurance.

I am desperate. You are fulfillment.

I am confused. You are confidence.

I am tired. You are rejuvenation.

Though the long path is uncertain, You are so faithful to shed just enough light for me to see the very next step. I now understand this isn't You being mysterious. This is a great demonstration of Your mercy.

Too much revelation and I'd pridefully run ahead of You. Too little and I'd be paralyzed with fear.

So, I'm seeking slivers of light in Your Truth just for today and filling the gaps of my unknown with trust.

Chapter 6

↬

Friendship Breakups

You know what I secretly hope for in my friendships? For my "I" to turn into a "we." And for the "we" connection to be a final destination where, from this point on, I sign off on each day with a lovely little, "and we are still living happily ever after."

I want the equation to be: make a friend, keep a friend. Live in a blissful place of fun connection. See eye to eye. Believe the best. Get along. Be nice. Collect hilarious inside jokes along the way. And fight for each other always.

That's what I secretly hope for. But that's not reality. Sometimes the equation is make a friend, try your best with that friend, and things go cold. Really cold.

That's where I was when I sat on the edge of my bed, staring down at my phone contacts list. There's a disturbing little button at the end of the edit option. While all other options are written in letters dressed in blue and green, this one is red. It stands out as red always does. It's at the very end, after scrolling through all other options and possibilities.

Two red words. I touched them with my pointer finger. And then, almost as if my phone was reminding me to exhaust all other options first, it made me double confirm this really was my intended action.

It was.

Because she told me she no longer wished to have any connection with me and I needed to respect this, I hit the red-lettered request again.

Delete contact.

We'd both tried. But there was an accumulating tension with each misunderstanding. Almost like an archer pulling back on a bow. The more it's pulled, the more the tension increases. At some point the archer will have to release the tension by releasing the arrow. I was so hoping the arrow would hit the bull's-eye of forgiveness and restoration. But that's not where the arrow went. The tension released. The arrow flew. And it wound up deeply piercing us both.

I'd love to paint some version of this where I present all I did to try and give and forgive. I think I could really impress you with quite an array of brushstrokes and colors. But in the end, one-sided views make for pretty flat-looking works of art.

She has her own version, and to deny that would make me guilty of more than just losing a friendship. It would further complicate things with selfishness.

I have to boss myself around in this. Denying myself the pleasure of presenting proof and building a case isn't easy. It's quite maddening, in fact. I imagine you, like me, have a few file folders of good proof that build a solid case that we are in fact *right! Justified! Not guilty!*

Bang the gavel. Be declared winner. Pump my fist. Feel so vindicated. Walk out victorious. But let's be honest. You've got two pierced souls, a friendship that ended, and a contact now deleted. Is there ever really a winner in a case like this?

People who care more about being right than ending right prove just how wrong they were all along. Lord, let me end this the right way.

People who care more about being right than ending right prove just how wrong they were all along.

The fragile nature of my heart needs time. So I give it just that. They say time heals—and I think this can be true—but only if that's truly the goal here: healing. Time grows the seeds that are planted, watered, and fertilized. Plant beauty, grow beauty. Plant thorns, grow thorns. Time will allow for either.

At this point I'm compelled to reach across this page, grab your hand, and say, "Bitterness, resentment, and anger have no place in a heart as beautiful as yours." I say it, because I need to hear it too.

So, I give this whole thing time. And I have to fight through sometimes wanting to fight back. Especially when I don't think God is telling her the same challenging "end right, end well" messages He's telling me.

It's distracting and messy and so very hard. The roots of

Bitterness,
resentment,
and anger have
no place in a heart as
beautiful as yours.

this friendship that once nourished me in deep places now ache with a barren flow. The conversations and connections have been hollowed out and replaced with a stabbing throb of a pierced soul. The arrow dug deep.

How is it possible to live loved in this? How is it possible to bring the fullness of God into a situation that seems so fully dead? But then one day this terrible, wonderful notion popped into my head: *Fight for her.*

This felt terrible to my flesh: *Excuse me while I lie on a couch and talk to a high-priced person with a degree hanging on her wall and a notepad in her hand. It's time for a professional. Clearly, things are not right in my head.*

But the notion of fighting for her felt wonderfully life-giving to my soul. I asked the notion, "Are you Jesus? And did you in fact just say 'fight for her'? Because I've been working my soul to the bone trying not to fight. End right. Remember?"

Fight for her.

That's it. That's all that kept rumbling about in my heart.

I rewound the tape all the way back to when I stood with a file folder full of my proof, denying myself the pleasure of presenting a case in my favor. I realized though I hadn't allowed myself to voice my case, this proof had become my secret treasure. I would quietly revisit it sometimes to privately enjoy it. But just as with any secret treat, just because no one sees you eat it doesn't mean the calories don't affect you. Being right tastes good but isn't worth the bloating it causes.

Fight for her.

I didn't have any sort of clarity as to why I was having this notion or even how to carry this out. But I remembered

Ephesians 6:12, and it seemed to fit: "For our struggle is not against flesh and blood, but against the rulers, against the authorities, against the powers of this dark world and against the spiritual forces of evil in the heavenly realms."

Before we go any further, let me clearly state a few of my feelings:

I very much feel like my struggle is against her.

I have been deeply hurt by this struggle.

It's hard to see that my struggle isn't with her or caused by her.

Those are my feelings.

But truth seems to want to help me get to a better place. Truth says I have an enemy but it's not really her. She may very well be the cause of some hurt in my life, but she's not my enemy. And I may very well be the cause of some hurt in her life, but I'm not her enemy.

We have an enemy, and it's not each other.

I point my crosshairs at the real enemy and start firing off positive statements about my friend. I list three things about her that are absolutely terrific. Then I remember a fourth and a fifth. I picture each of these positive statements wounding the Devil as this hits him squarely where he's most vulnerable. Truth proclaimed and lived out is a fiercely accurate weapon against evil.

None of this untangles the issues in this broken relationship. Nor have I added her back into my contacts list.

But it did help me reestablish a "we" here. We have a common enemy. I have a choice to see that or not. To live truth or not. To fight for her and against the real enemy or not. So I list out positive things six and seven. And I make my choice.

Is any of this easy? No, not at all. It's so very hard. But it's good for my soul to get to this place. It keeps me in a place of acknowledging God as God. It's saying: *I don't know all the details entangled in this issue. But You know all. Therefore, You, God, are the only One who can handle all. There are a lot of things my flesh is tempted to seek—fairness, my right to be right, proof of her wrongdoing, to make her see things from my vantage point—but at this point, the only thing healthy for me to seek is You. You alone. I'm going to be obedient to You and let You handle everything else.*

This is what it looks like to rise above the circumstances and determine to hold on to the greater good in the grand scheme of things: honoring God.

We do so by remembering our job is to be obedient to God. God's job is everything else.

We must speak with honor in the midst of being
   dishonored.
We must speak with peace in the midst of being
   threatened.
We must speak of good things in the midst of a bad
   situation.
We must be obedient to, trust, and believe God and let
   Him boss around our contrary feelings.

Remember how we've talked about "living loved" and "bringing the fullness of God" into any situation? This is it. And it's really the only way to get to the place where we can have peace in a situation that doesn't have a storybook ending.

So I fight for her.

Not because we will reconnect. We haven't. And we might not.

Not because she's right.

Not because I'm right.

I fight for her simply because I want to stay right in step with honoring God.

Chapter 7

≈

When Our Normal
Gets Snatched

My mouth was dry. My hands a bit numb. There was a stabbing tightness in my chest. My mind blurred as my thoughts became a fragmented kaleidoscope of a million pictured hopes I thought were just around the corner for me. For us. For the us that was now becoming just me again.

We were only dating. But my mind had already run ahead in time and built a life with this man. In the future we had romantic picnics to take, snowball fights to laugh through, a wedding to plan, a house to build, and kids to name who had his smile and my eyes.

I'm not sure these were ever real to him. But to me, they were as real as the stone-cold coffee now sitting in front of me. The one I kept stirring to have something to focus on but that I never intended to drink. Drinking coffee seemed a bit too normal of an activity to participate in when my entire inner life had just been declared a state of emergency.

Because all of a sudden, the rest of my planned-out life was aflame. I wasn't just losing a boyfriend today. I was losing the connection to all those dreams for tomorrow that now would never be.

His words were making their way through my ears to my heart.

I felt the full impact of their harsh landing. As they skidded their way across the most tender places inside me, their piercing weight burned and cut and ripped apart what I thought would be so very permanent. Rejection always leaves the deepest, darkest marks.

That was more than twenty-five years ago. But I can pull up the memory of it as if it were yesterday. I have to search around a bit in my past, but there it is. The wound isn't pulsing with pain any longer. It's more of a scar. Like a war wound, it's just a story now.

At first, though, not even in sleep could I escape it. Even if I was fortunate enough not to dream about it, I'd wake up devastated afresh as soon as reality tumbled in past the edges of my sleep. I'd relive this over and over until stabbing moments turned into days turned into weeks turned into enough time for this to slowly move from reality to a memory to a place called my past.

I pulled out my journal today and tried to capture the raw essence of what makes rejection so awful. But in the end I couldn't capture the depth of it with finely crafted words. Instead of diving deep with my thoughts, I let them come in simple, personal phrases.

I like stability.

I don't like getting caught off guard.

I like feeling known.

I don't like feeling thrown away.

I like for people to believe the best about me.

I don't like being misunderstood.

I like feeling that my presence draws people close.

I don't like feeling that they saw me but pretended they didn't.

I like to be liked.

I don't like to be left out or walked away from.

I like feeling that this person is my person.

I don't like knowing this person was my person but is not any longer.

As I kept making this list, one line finally emerged that seemed to sum up rejection better than the others: *I don't want my normal to be snatched away.* Life feels impossibly risky when I'm reminded how unpredictable circumstances can shatter and forever change what I know and love about my life. And in the fallout, some pieces never find a way to fall back into place.

It's like taking a photograph containing all the people you love and suddenly some of those people purposely cut themselves out of the picture. And the gaping hole left behind is in some ways worse than death. If their absence was caused by death, you would grieve their loss. But when their absence is caused by rejection, you not only grieve their loss but you also have to wrestle through the fact that they wanted this. They chose to cut themselves out.

Though you are devastated, they are possibly walking away

feeling relieved. Or worse, they might even feel happy. And there you sit, staring at a jacked-up photograph that no glue in the world can fix. Normal has been taken. Not by accident. But very much on purpose by someone you never expected could be such a thief.

Because *rejection* is an abstract word that doesn't have an image attached to it, I couldn't fully see all of this until I witnessed something last Christmas in a department store. When a thief snatched normal right out from the midst of an otherwise typical day.

The sound of the woman screaming reached my ears quicker than the realization of what was happening. A man bolted out the exit door right beside us. A woman wearing leather boots fresh out of the box ran after him. Her panicked calls for help alarmed a shoes salesman who then ran out just behind her.

A crowd gathered at the door, murmuring and collectively putting together pieces of information about what was happening. Apparently the woman had been trying on boots in this nice store with chairs and full-length mirrors and friendly salespeople. Christmas music was in the air. Sale signs were on the racks. And happiness hovered about like the laughter of children on a playground.

My daughter and I were looking at a pair of shoes, discussing them as a possible gift for a family friend. And that's when it happened.

Like a needle scratching all the way across a record, signaling time to stand still and people to hold their breaths. A man had obviously been watching, waiting, casing this scene.

And then the woman with the boots took two steps toward a mirror, turned, and just like that her purse was being carried off by a stranger. Now she was screaming down a sidewalk, and everything about her day was in unexpected disarray.

I walked over to where she'd been sitting a minute before and stared down at her left-behind jacket and the shoes she'd worn into the store. I didn't know this woman. I'm not sure I'd even noticed her standing near us. She was just another face in the crowd, a blur of background as I went about my agenda. But now I felt oddly connected to this stranger and determined to protect her remaining belongings. I stood guard in this place where her normal got snatched.

And it felt strangely sacred.

Because I so relate to life splitting open and snatching normal right out from underneath me. And I stood there staring in as much disbelief as the woman now coming back inside the store, still wearing the leather boots fresh out of the box.

In the end she lost only her cell phone. The thief, not thinking a screaming woman would chase him, wound up tossing her purse aside and just taking the phone before escaping from all the commotion.

I walked over and handed her the jacket and well-worn shoes she'd left behind. I wished her well. And then I wished I could also run down the sidewalk screaming the next time my normal gets snatched. I wished life would change its mind, tossing most of what I lost back to me. But that's not the way things always work out.

Sometimes things taken stay gone.

I've had my heart broken enough to know this very well.

Too many of us have.

Like my friend whose husband decided he'd had enough of

her and not enough of another woman who'd caught his eye. She had heard the devastating words no wife ever wants to hear, and now she was watching the movers pack up the life she loved.

A few hours into the process of emptying her home, the movers carried out her wedding portrait and called to her, "You want the photographs in the stairwell to go with us, or are you taking those separately in your vehicle?"

"I'll be taking those separately," she said, the irony not escaping her. Separately. That was how she'd be living her life now. Separate from the neighborhood where her kids had grown up. Separate from her husband. Separate from the way she thought her life would be.

She took the wedding portrait from the mover as a feeling of confusion washed over her. She sat down on the front steps and called me. Through her tears she said, "I don't know what to do with this portrait. What do you do with the things that have no place anymore? We built a life together, and now there's no more together. There isn't a place for that in my mind. What am I going to do?"

Her normal had been snatched. And it wasn't just her wedding portrait that seemed to have no place. Everything felt strange and hard and different and impossibly irreversible. I guess this is at the core of why rejection stings in waves over and over again. There's a loss of what was and what we thought would be. What was normal is snatched, and no amount of screaming and running down a sidewalk will get it back.

And it's not just the thing taken that haunts us. It's the reality that humans can be vicious and selfish and cruel. That's what rejection does. Rejection steals the security of all we thought was beautiful and stable and leaves us scared and fragile and more vulnerable than ever.

Suddenly, what I saw in the store that day isn't about a stranger's purse. It's about my friend's husband rejecting her. It's about another friend who took the piece of my heart I entrusted to her and stopped calling me back. And my dad, who was unable to stay. And that teacher who called my daughter out into the hallway and told her she was a bad, bad, bad girl until she slumped into a puddle of tears.

I ball my hand into a fist as the words, "how dare you," form in my mouth. The needed justice is sweet to my tongue and satisfying to my palate. I start to develop a craving for malice.

But God. He's there.

The One whom I proclaimed is good. Good to me. Good at being God.

The One with whom I am living a love story.

And I know I can't continue to fully embrace God while rejecting His ways.

I can't continue to fully embrace
God while rejecting His ways.

God drops a word into my heart. Like a swig of orange juice just after brushing my teeth, I recoil at the unexpected taste. Of grace.

Grace!

Why grace?!

Grace given when it feels least deserved is the only antidote for bitter rot.

I picture myself standing between two boxes. From one the stench is unbearably brutal, bellowing out dark wisps of death. And the other box is full of white lilies. Their angelic blooms are fully stretched and sending out perfume, sweet and pure.

A box of bitterness. A box of grace.

Looking at these boxes helps me see the horrible in bitterness and the honorable in grace. Seeing and smelling bitterness doesn't make it nearly as appealing. I lift the orange juice and take another swig and discover I like it more this time. The more I drink, the more I crave this taste.

"Not now" grace soon turns into "right now" grace. I realize if I don't cooperate with grace in this moment, for this thief, for that friend, for my dad, and for that teacher . . . I will carry the stench of the bitter box and rub it off on all who come close to me. And this realization makes me so annoyed.

I'm the one who was hurt, and now I have to be the one to be the bigger person? The thief, friend, father, and teacher should be the ones to pluck the bouquet of lilies from the good-smelling box, arrange them with ferns and little white sprigs of baby's breath, put them in a glass vase, and deliver them to my front doorstep. With chocolates. And deep, heaving sobs of repentance. While sporting the worst haircut of their lives and the fifteen pounds of which I'd love to be rid.

Yes!

Now things are starting to feel a little more fair.

But seeking what's fair never cracked the world open to reveal the beautiful reality of a Jesus-loving woman. Only a pure heart with space for grace can do that. Indeed, grace is such a crazy notion to the heart of the one rejected. But if we will step over the hurt feelings and turn from the box of bitter rot, we are then free to pick up the box of sweet, pure lilies.

We can form bouquets to give away.

We will linger with the smell of one who spends time with her fingers working through grace.

We will see a tweaking of our souls in the midst of things taken that stayed gone. We prove that not everyone in this world is vicious and selfish and cruel. And we even dare to pray for the thief, friend, father, and teacher. For at some point in their lives, someone took from them and left them screaming on a sidewalk.

There's nothing we can do to eliminate rejection. Oh, how I wish there were. With every fiber of my being, I wish I could remove it from my world and from yours. But I can't. The only thing I've seen work in my life to protect my heart from these deep wounds is the constant pursuit of the sweetest grace.

To love God is to cooperate with His grace. And since I'm so very aware of my own need for grace, I must be willing to freely give it away. Each hole left from rejection must become an opportunity to create more and more space for grace in my heart.

---

*To love God is to cooperate
with His grace.*

There is a woman named Abigail in 1 Samuel 25 who had to decide between grace and bitterness. Abigail was a woman well acquainted with hardship, negative people, rejection, and things not turning out as I'm sure she wished they would.

But somehow she remained steady. And her steadiness proved to have a profound impact on the life of David. This is the David who defeated Goliath, who became the king of Israel, who, though he fell and faltered many times, God said was a man after His own heart. This David is the one from whose bloodline King Jesus would come.

Abigail isn't talked about or heralded much today. I'm not sure why. When everyone else arrives in heaven and is clamoring to have coffee with the saints of old, she's one who will be at the top of my list. I feel pretty certain we are destined to be BFFs. Of course, she doesn't know this, so if you get there before me, please don't tell her and make her think I fall in the creeper-stalker category.

But seriously, I adore this woman.

She was married to a fool named Nabal—his name literally means "fool" in Hebrew—who had deeply offended David.

David and his men had served Nabal by protecting his herds, and since it was a feast day, he sent Nabal a message asking for his "favor," requesting special festive food. The Hebrew root word for *favor* here is *chen*, which also means "grace."

But Nabal denied David. He didn't give him food. And he certainly didn't give him favor or grace. Instead, he responded with an infuriating rejection of David and his men. David, in turn, vowed to kill Nabal and all the males belonging to him.

Obviously this horrible situation caused by her husband's careless words deeply affected Abigail. And it wasn't just this event that seemed so hard on her. I'm sure Nabal's cruelty and foolishness spilled in her direction more often than anyone else's. She probably felt rejected again and again in her marriage. And then again and again by the people who wanted nothing to do with the wife of such a foolish man.

But instead of filling up this rejected space with insecurity, she found stability by filling it with grace. The more she hurt, the more she learned how to help others who were hurt.

In this situation, she figured out a way to give David not only festive food but also the kindness Nabal had denied him. She gave to him out of her own lack, from the empty places in her heart that God so graciously filled. With an enormous space for grace, she approached David, the man about to kill her family and her servants, and she quickly bowed down before him.

I want this. But, boy, is it hard to live like this in the heated moment of hurt. I'm stunned by how well Abigail lived this. I find myself trying to resist grace in her story. After all, her first words to David seem so beyond what my own feelings would have allowed in this situation: "On me alone, my lord, be the blame" (1 Samuel 25:24 NASB).

I read this and clench my jaw. I've grown so fond of her I absolutely refuse to be okay with her owning any part of this.

Cast the blame on Nabal. He's the jerk in this story.

Or place the blame on David. He's the hot-headed one here. But not Abigail.

She's already had to wrestle under the weight of an unfair life. Now she has to step in between her ridiculous husband and a hungry, crazed David to take on blame that clearly wasn't hers to bear?

She's the victim. She's the one who, in the middle of getting ready for a festival, had normal ripped right out from her midst. One minute she's making out her Target and Hobby Lobby errands list, and the next minute a servant comes and announces disaster is hanging over her household. But instead of bowing to anger, cynicism, blame—all too often the fruits of living rejected—she chooses grace.

How did she process this in such a healthy way? Had she some tweaking of the soul? Some vision of the bitter box reeking of rot that deterred her from walking toward it? I don't know these details. But I do see an immediate cooperation with grace.

Her giving grace doesn't justify her husband or validate David.

It saves her.

It makes David stop cold in his heated tracks.

It makes the men, pulsing with swords in their hands and death on their minds, pause. I can almost see their arms full of weapons and their bodies full of testosterone tremble. What a scene. Though Abigail is bowed low, grace gives her the upper hand. She refuses to be a victim of a circumstance she can't fully change. Instead she changes what she can.

It's impossible to hold up the banners of victim and victory at the same time. With victory in mind, she bows low before David and, with great courage, allows the mantle of blame to be placed on her shoulders. After all, she's the only one strong enough to handle it.

The humiliation of being married to a man named Fool had secretly worked something good deep within Abigail's soul. The more she cooperated with grace, the more her humiliation turned into humility. Humility can't be bought at a bargain price. It's the long working of grace upon grace within the hurts of our hearts.

Humility gave Abigail the greatest advantage in this life-and-death conversation with David. Humility opens the ears of opportunity.

In the next chapter we will unpack her amazing conversation with David. Abigail's grace-filled words are what I believe to be one of the greatest speeches of the Bible. After all, here we sit talking about it thousands of years later. And instead of the screams from a sidewalk, it's her words that echo into the deep places of our hearts.

It's *impossible* to

hold up the banners

of *victim*

and *victory* at

the same time.

Chapter 8

❧

The Corrective Experience

I got an e-mail this morning that made my heart sink. "I am turning in my resignation, because I do not agree with the new direction you are taking our committee. I shared my thoughts at the last meeting, but it is obvious you and I see things differently."

Ouch.

What a major bummer to wake up to. Especially because when I talked to this fellow committee member last week, I thought we were really starting to see eye to eye.

Due to budget cuts, we needed to change some of our original plans for the school event we were organizing. But this didn't sit well with this person. She wanted to charge more for the tickets to cover the extra cost. I totally understood her point. We had worked really hard on our original plan, and this change would cause us to have to go back to the drawing board, putting a lot more work on us.

So, yes, I understood her frustration. But as I processed requiring people to pay more, I realized some parents wouldn't be able to afford this change. And I didn't want anyone to have to tell her kids they couldn't come because of the cost. I recommended scaling back our plans rather than having some kids be unable to attend.

I thought she agreed with me. But apparently, from her latest e-mail, she didn't. And on top of that, I got the distinct impression she was quite angry and frustrated with me.

I put my head down on the kitchen table and sighed.

I had woken up happy and ready to regroup with my committee to make the best of a hard budget situation. It was already going to be a challenge to do what needed to be done, but I'd rallied in my heart and believed we could get creative and things would still turn out just fine. Now I just felt defeated.

Every bit of my creative energy started draining out of what felt like holes drilled into my heart. I was trying to do a good thing volunteering to lead this committee, but now I felt all it had done was add drama to my life. I started questioning, *Am I bad leader? Do the other members want to resign too? What if they all quit and I'm left to do this alone? I can't do this alone!*

What started off as a day full of potential turned into me feeling like a rejected failure. All from one e-mail. Good gracious.

I pressed the sides of my head and willed my eyes to refuse the production of tears. I felt horrible. And then mad. And then penned in by circumstances beyond my control. But most of all I just felt incredibly misunderstood. *Should I call the writer of the e-mail and try to talk it through some more? Or just leave it alone? Ugh, why do I care so much? Of course I should care so much!* It all just felt like a tangled mess.

I wish I could tell you that this was an isolated situation. But these kinds of tangled messes seem to go hand in hand with trying to get different people on the same page. Different people with differing perspectives will find themselves in difficult situations unless they determine to discuss things well.

Relationships don't come in packages of perfection; relationships come in packages of potential. They have the potential to be great. But they also have the potential to be hard at times. No matter what, it takes work to make it work. And wrapped in between the wonderful and the work are inevitable times of imperfection and possible rejection.

That's just part of it. But I'm determined to examine how I can have better conversations in the future when differing opinions are involved. The first thing I realize I could have done better in this situation was to start from a "me too" place rather than from a "you should" or "you could" place.

This "me too" says to the other person, "I hear you and I see the validity in your feelings, because I've had those feelings before too."

A couple of years ago, I was helping a friend with some book-writing tips. As I read his first chapter, I realized he was writing in a way that would not draw the reader in because he jumped right into preaching and teaching. As a reader, I didn't need that. I needed a friend who understood the struggle being addressed in the book.

If writers don't show me their struggles, I can't trust their advice. I don't want theories that smell like a library; I want advice to smell like it has some real life in it. I want to know what they are writing about has worked on their own issues so I can believe it might work on mine.

Take away the struggle, and you take away my trust. I

Relationships

don't come

in packages

of *perfection*;

relationships come in

packages of *potential*.

advised my writing friend to shift his approach from "you should" or "you could" to "me too." And it made all the difference in his book feeling more accessible and approachable. Maybe the same is true when having a difficult conversation with someone of a differing opinion. If I approach that person first with a "you should" attitude, it will feel like I'm wagging my finger and preaching at her.

"You should consider . . ."

"You should think of . . ."

"You should have more compassion for . . ."

"You should have told me . . ."

"You should have never . . ."

This will instantly put her on the defensive and bait her to build a case against me. This happens when I'm more concerned about making my point than making progress. And almost worse, if I approach her with a "you could" attitude, it will feel like I'm trying to teach her a lesson that I'm not willing to apply myself.

"You could be more willing to . . ."

"You could think of this differently by . . ."

"You could be more sensitive to . . ."

"You could stop this . . ."

"You could start that . . ."

This will instantly position me as the expert and her as the less experienced student. When put in this unwelcomed position, people usually withdraw, shut down, and, in the case of my friend on the committee, resign.

Ugh. I hadn't meant to assume she needed me to teach her a lesson about being sensitive to other parents' finances. I was just passionate about helping her think of this situation from all sides. But, obviously, the "you should" or "you could" approach wasn't working.

"Me too" puts us on the same team. It says, "We are in this together, so let's attack the problem, not each other." Now, just as a point of clarification, saying "me too" must come with three guidelines of what this is *not* meant to do:

- It is not a tactic we should use to steal the spotlight. It's not saying, "Oh, me too. Now let's process all my hurt."
- It is not something we should use to one-up their hurt. It's not saying, "Me, too, except if you think what you're going through is difficult, let me show you what real difficulties are."
- And lastly, it is not a validation of their actions that spring from their feelings. It's simply acknowledging their feelings and identifying with them if you can authentically do that.

Abigail is also such a good example of "me too" done right. In 1 Samuel 25, she was brilliant in her approach with David. She acknowledged right away that her husband had acted foolishly toward him. But the way she said it let David know Abigail was a victim of Nabal's foolishness as well. "His name is fool and folly goes with him everywhere he goes" (1 Samuel 25:25, paraphrased).

This was Abigail's "me too" statement. Though she didn't use the words *me too,* she certainly used the sentiment of this powerful two-word statement. By stating that folly goes with Nabal everywhere, she made it clear that Nabal's foolishness wasn't just directed at David. It flowed in every direction of his life and impacted everyone with whom he interacted. And by "everywhere" she clearly meant in his home and with her.

A woman's eyes often hold conversations within their stare. And I imagine Abigail's eyes gently communicated some version of these statements:

He's treated you poorly, David.
Me too. I understand.
He didn't think about caring for you, David.
Me too. I understand.
He didn't appreciate what you'd done for him, David.
Me too. I understand.

And she brilliantly knew something else as well. She knew David wasn't looking for a lesson. He was looking for food and respect. Before addressing his issues, she came prepared to acknowledge his need. Even this was a "me too" statement.

You feel you and your men more than deserve festive food in return for your kindness in watching Nabal's flocks?

Me too. I agree you and your men deserve food.

The second thing I'm beginning to realize as I process a better way of communication is clearly stating "you do belong."

"Me too" communicates to a person she is understood.

"You do belong" communicates she is accepted.

Acceptance is like an antibiotic that prevents past rejections from turning into present-day infections. The need for belonging runs deep.

The need to belong goes beyond the need for superficial social ties . . . it is a need for meaningful, profound bonding.

Acceptance is like an antibiotic that prevents past rejections from turning into present-day infections.

A sense of belongingness is crucial to our well-being . . . The lack of belongingness causes various undesirable effects, including a decrease in the levels of health, happiness, and adjustment.[1]

I believe what pushed my committee member to respond by immediately resigning was the sudden feeling her ideas were no longer heard and, therefore, she didn't have a place on our team. No more feeling of contribution, no more feeling of belonging. And maybe this wasn't the first time she'd felt that way.

Most of us have been made to feel like we don't belong at some point in our lives. It's a bummer to be left out, not chosen, and overlooked. But when someone of great significance in our lives makes us feel like our belonging is more of a question mark than a security blanket, we become very sensitive to even the slightest hints of rejection. The wound is reopened, and rejection's infection sets in.

For David, it wasn't just that Nabal rejected his request for food. Nabal rejected him as a person and a leader.

"Who is this David? Who is this son of Jesse? Many servants are breaking away from their masters these days. Why should I take my bread and water, and the meat I have slaughtered for my shearers, and give it to men coming from who knows where?"

David's men turned around and went back. When they
arrived, they reported every word. (1 Samuel 25:10–12)

Nabal's dismissal of David conveyed:

You are not known.
You don't belong.
You aren't important.
You are not valuable.
You are not secure.

The minute David's men recounted Nabal's jarring words,
David went from a man hungry for food and recognition to a
man hungry for revenge. His reaction was quick, aggressive,
and extreme. Too extreme, don't you think?

I mean, after all, David was denied the equivalent of a
hamburger and water. And he's ready to kill over that? But it
really wasn't about the food at all. Extreme reactors are usually dealing with compounding factors. Nabal's words struck
an existing wound. Nabal wasn't the originator of David's
wound, but he certainly hit it dead on when he rejected David
and his request.

I believe the deep wound was caused years before by David's
father, Jesse. In 1 Samuel 16, when the prophet Samuel went to
Jesse, asking him to bring before him all his sons, he did just
that, with one exception. He left David out in the field. Either
he had totally forgotten about David or he held him in such
disregard that he never thought David had a chance to be the
chosen one. Why bring him in?

Either way, that's hurtful.

Jesse had seven of his sons pass before Samuel, but Samuel

said to him, "The LORD has not chosen these." He asked Jesse, "Are these all the sons you have?"

"There is still the youngest," Jesse answered. "But he . . ."

I won't put assumptions in Jesse's words. I know what he goes on to say: "He is tending the sheep."[2]

However, I think this is one of the lamest excuses he could give for not including David in what surely was the biggest event this family had ever taken part in. If David's father had any regard for his youngest son at all, he could have found someone else to temporarily tend the sheep.

I suspect that behind that statement were some thoughts like: *Well, yes, I have one more son—the youngest, David. But he . . . doesn't look like a king, doesn't act like a king, doesn't smell like a king. So, I didn't invite him.*

Uninvited by his own father.

Can you imagine how David must have felt when they finally went to get him and he stumbled into this event fresh from the field? *Dad brought everyone else but me.* And with an emotional dagger steaming with red-hot rejection, David's father inflicted a mark on his heart that read, "You don't belong."

You don't matter as much as your brothers.

You aren't important enough to be remembered.

You are not valuable enough to be considered.

You are not secure with this family who disregards you.

Even though Samuel went on to anoint David as the future king, I can't find where Jesse ever tended to his son's heart. Isn't it crazy that on the same day David achieved the ultimate success of being named the future king, he was overlooked by his father? No amount of outside achievement fixes inside hurts. Those hurts have to be soothed by replacing the lies with truth.

---

*No amount of outside achievement
fixes inside hurts.*

Can't you just hear Satan's cackle as Nabal pokes at that same wound still pulsing with pain from David's father's rejection? But then the ominous screams of evil give way to the sweet harmony of healing through Abigail.

When Abigail talked with David, she did the exact opposite of what Nabal did. And the opposite of what Jesse did. She reinstated a feeling of belonging in David. Her words were gentle, honoring, and life-giving. And most of all they were filled with God's truth.

> "Please forgive your servant's presumption. The LORD your God will certainly make a lasting dynasty for my lord, because you fight the LORD's battles, and no wrongdoing will be found in you as long as you live. Even though someone is pursuing you to take your life, the life of my lord will be bound securely in the bundle of the living by the LORD your God, but the lives of your enemies he will hurl away as from the pocket of a sling." (1 Samuel 25:28–29)

She spoke her words of truth in the tone of grace. After all, remember David was leading a mob of four hundred men with drawn swords to kill Nabal and all the males who belonged to him. And there were two hundred others who had stayed back to watch the supplies but were just as thirsty for a bloody revenge. But that's not who David was at his core. David was a man who belonged to God. Abigail spoke to who he was, not to how he was acting in the moment:

- You are a fighter of the Lord's battles. *(You are known. You matter to the Lord.)*
- The Lord has a plan for your dynasty to last. *(You are important.)*
- Someone is pursuing you to take your life, but God has a plan to keep you safe. *(You are valuable.)*
- Remember what God did when you hurled that stone from the pocket of a sling toward Goliath. God was faithful that day and is faithful this day too! *(You are secure.)*

Abigail soothed the deep wound Nabal had reopened.

In counseling terms this is called "the corrective experience." She revisited the hurt place of David's heart with healing words that corrected or rewrote the lies that had wounded him so deeply. (Be sure to check out the Corrective Experience Chart on pages 230–31 to apply this to your life.)

Did Abigail know of David's wound? There's a chance she'd heard of Jesse's actions toward David on the day of his anointing. He wasn't an anonymous figure; he was the future king. And she makes it clear during her speech that she knew his royal destiny. But what she saw herself was that David's reaction surely had more hurt behind it than simply what Nabal had caused.

Isn't that true of most of us? If we react with more emotion than is appropriate for an isolated incident, it's probably not so isolated. The escalated emotion of this situation is probably an indication of painful ties to the past. I believe this was true of David.

Where David's father and Nabal had spoken death, with divinely inspired words Abigail spoke life. Each of her statements called forth the truth of his identity and quieted the lies of the enemy. And, as a result, he changed.

He felt safe enough to listen to her. He felt safe enough to take the food she'd brought him. He felt safe enough to turn back to his men and retract the plan he'd so boldly declared to kill Nabal. And most of all, he felt safe enough to believe and receive God's message through Abigail.

"Me too" and "you do belong" are powerful words. Not just for Abigail and David but for all of us. These are soothing statements that calm and heal, beautiful realities for us to receive from God personally and believe. And they are incredible truths to stick in our back pockets as gifts to be given in conversations with others.

Let your past rejection experiences work *for* you instead of *against* you by allowing them to help you sense the possible pain behind other people's reactions. Try to see things from their vantage points and think of how they might be hurting in this situation. Even if you don't agree with their stance or their reaction, find a way to identify with their hurt. Most people are walking around with way more hurts from their past than we can ever imagine. Pretty much everyone has at some point been deeply hurt by someone. That's your "me too."

Then make a list of good things you know to be true about that person like I did in chapter 6. This doesn't validate her actions in the moment, but it will validate her worth as a person. Even if you are clueless about the past hurts that could be feeding her reaction, you can still be sensitive to her obvious pain. You will be an agent of grace in her life as you whisper, "You do belong."

And all of this will help you to stop the cycle of rejection and hurt.

In the other person's life.

And in your life.

On that note, I guess now I'll go respond to that resignation e-mail. I don't know everything I'll say, but you bet "me too" and "you do belong" will now be part of it.

Chapter 9

Chapter 9

❧

Why Does Rejection
Hurt So Much?

L ysa, we have to go in a different direction than we origi-
nally thought. We saw your great potential, but there was
another candidate better qualified for this opportunity."

Silence.

Complete and utter silence hung in the air as my brain refused to bring forth anything appropriate to say. I had to be
professional. I didn't want to further validate their obvious
doubt about me. And I knew I'd regret doing anything that
betrayed my relationship with Jesus.

But I wasn't feeling very spiritually motivated in this moment
of utter shock.

They'd already committed to me.

I'd told people. I'd posted about it on social media. I'd been
so excited.

And now, in one unexpected phone call, this opportunity I'd been so excited about was shut down. With a total display of brilliance and intelligence, I uttered, "Okay, um, sure, well, okay."

There was an awkward exchange of pleasantries and something about the weather and a totally flat-sounding promise of being in touch with me about future projects. And that was that.

My hands and lips felt completely numb. I brushed at the crumbs on the table. I picked at a hangnail until it bled, willing it to make me feel something other than the stabbing sensation in my chest.

I wanted to cry. But I didn't want to cry. I wanted to scream. Only I definitely didn't want to scream. I wanted to call them back and beg for their reconsideration. However, I absolutely didn't want to call them back and beg for anything!

I wondered if I might be teetering on the edge of a panic attack. Should I get a brown paper bag and breathe in some sort of calming rhythm? I'd have to YouTube the details on this. I clearly was handling this like a champ. And it seemed my reaction only further confirmed why I totally should have been rejected by them, which only made me feel worse.

I wish I could say I got up and went for a run. Or read my Bible. Or went to pull weeds. Something productive that I could later cheer about and say, "Yay, me. Look how well you handled that."

But no.

Instead, I hopped on the Internet to see if I could figure out who they'd chosen over me. My brain kept saying to *stop this right now*! But my curiosity and fingers wouldn't cooperate. And it didn't take long for me to see in pixilated detail her perfect smile, confident stance, and impressive list of accomplishments. And, though they hired her for her Bible brilliance and probably never even noticed her thin legs, I totally noticed.

Of course she had thin legs. Salt in my worst wound!

Her jeans didn't appear to pull and beg for mercy like mine do on the regular. And I'm certain hers didn't have those little fabric pills on the inner thigh region, because she had—hold the phone—a slight thigh gap.

The thigh gap did me in.

Totally.

Don't judge me. I'm not at all a proponent of thigh gaps. As a matter of fact, I'm against them. Totally. It's quite obvi-ous . . . Lord, have mercy on all that jiggles on me. And my soul. And my obviously whacked-out brain.

Time for rationality to kick in.

I stood at my full-length mirror and tried to manipulate a thigh gap. If I turned my toes in just so and pushed my back-side out a tad and begged my hips to pretend to adjust to an unrealistic angle and forced my knees to bow, then voilà! For one brief millisecond a sliver of light appeared. But my inner thighs have some sort of magnetic attraction determined to flop them back together. Like birds of a feather. Make that a fluffy feather.

I'm completely sane except when I'm the opposite of that.

This situation messed me up for days.

I felt utterly squashed inside my heart and squishier than ever around my thighs. Although, honestly, this had nothing at all to do with my thighs or hers. It just made me feel bet-ter to attribute being uninvited to something trivial, because then I simply roll my eyes at the shallowness of it all. But it wasn't for shallow reasons that I was uninvited. It was that the committee determined she was a better fit for their event.

And you know what really felt like an utter betrayal? I knew God could fix this, and He didn't.

Rejection is so incredibly painful.

> Rejection piggybacks on physical pain pathways in the brain. MRI studies show that the same areas of the brain become activated when we experience rejection as when we experience physical pain. This is why rejection hurts so much (neurologically speaking). In fact our brains respond so similarly to rejection and physical pain that Tylenol reduces the emotional pain rejection elicits. In a study testing the hypothesis that rejection mimics physical pain, researchers gave some participants acetaminophen (Tylenol) before asking them to recall a painful rejection experience. The people who received Tylenol reported significantly less emotional pain than subjects who took a sugar pill.[1]

Strange facts like this fascinate me. But it didn't comfort me. I was pretty sure no Tylenol would help. This went beyond just rejection from man. That is hard. But what's downright horrible is when God seems to just silently stand by, withholding answers and solutions for which you've cried out. That deep hurt can make you question His goodness.

This situation was small in comparison to other rejections I've faced. But it tapped into a raw emotional place of other unresolved hurts, a deep well holding tears from many other times someone had said, "You're not good enough."

Rejection isn't just an emotional feeling. It's a message that alters what you believe about yourself. And the minute you sense that happening is the minute you must stop the runaway thinking with truth.

I needed to shift my thinking, not only in order to process thigh-gap girl's success well, but also to make sure I didn't internalize a lie about my identity and then miss what God *was* doing here despite His seeming silence.

God is always at work. He is a present, loving Father, aware of our deepest hurts and our even deeper needs.

We aren't always able to see this clearly. Still, even when it seems otherwise, we must remember that sometimes when we feel rejected and passed over for someone else, when God seems busy elsewhere or even purposefully unmoving, the truth is He is at work, maybe doing something entirely beyond what we were thinking.

You Aren't Set Aside

Not too long after being uninvited to the conference I just told you about, I received an invitation to a leaders' gathering. I was so thankful. I just knew I'd be able to swap stories with the other attendees about their uninvited moments, and it would totally make me feel more normal.

Yes, there were many feelings I thought I'd have at this small conference I was so looking forward to attending. Acceptance. Fun. Camaraderie. On paper, these were my people.

They led organizations. I led an organization. They were vulnerable. I was vulnerable. Like me, they knew the public pressures that feed our private insecurities. They knew the stresses of deadlines, trying to balance kids with ministry, and the nagging sense that we should keep hidden the fact that we have the pizza-delivery place on speed dial.

Yes, these would for sure be my people. And the great thing about gathering with people with whom you just know you are going to bond, is that they will get you. Really get you—like on the level of having inside jokes that make every conversation comfortable and delightful.

I couldn't wait to be with these people. And I couldn't wait for the deep friendships that would surely bloom as a result of our time together. I walked into the room and quickly found the people I was excited to meet. Every seat had a name tag attached, so I circled the table, looking for mine. As I got to the last chair and realized my name wasn't there, I had a sinking feeling.

I milled around the room, looking for my name, feeling increasingly out of place. Finally, at a table on the opposite side of the room, I found it. I rallied in my heart that the Lord must have a special plan for me to meet and connect with the others assigned to my table. I took my seat and pulled out my cell phone, nervously waiting for my tablemates.

I waited.

And waited.

And waited.

As the prayer for the meal concluded and the event got well under way, it was painfully apparent the others assigned to my table weren't able to come for some reason. I'd be seated alone. Very alone.

In reality, I don't think anyone else really noticed my predicament. After all, by this point everyone in the room was busy passing rolls and salad dressing options. In my head I started to have a little pity conversation: *Well, self, would you like a roll? Or ten perhaps? It's certainly an option when you're sitting single at a table for ten.*

And that's when a very clear sentence popped into my head. *You aren't set aside, Lysa. You are set apart.* It wasn't audible. And it wasn't my own thought. I knew it was a thought assigned by God that I needed to ponder.

To be set aside is to be rejected.

That's exactly what the enemy would have wanted me to feel. If he could get me to feel this, then I'd become completely self-absorbed in my own insecurity and miss whatever the reason God had for me to be at this event.

To be set apart is to be given an assignment that requires preparation.

That's what I believe God wanted me to see. If He could get me to understand this, I'd be able to embrace the lesson of this situation. And the lesson of being uninvited from the other event. And just a solid lesson for life in general.

The lesson was this: Anything that infuses us with humility is good. Even if it feels a bit like humiliation in the moment, the workings of humility within are a gift.

The tweaking of us by God in the quiet is the saving of us in public. The only difference between humility and humiliation is that one chose to bow low while the other tripped and fell there. Either way, the sweetest grace lifted my face, and I saw that on the other side of the stripping of pride are some of the best gifts God gives us.

The Bible reminds us that on the other side of humility we find wisdom (Proverbs 11:2). We will be lifted up by God Himself in due time (1 Peter 5:6). "God opposes the proud but gives grace to the humble" (James 4:6 NLT). Humility isn't a place of weakness but rather a position that will come with

The tweaking

of us by God

in the quiet is

the saving of us

in public.

honor (Proverbs 18:12). And humility is an absolute requirement for those who ask God to heal their land (2 Chronicles 7:14).

Yes, rejection is humbling to the point of humiliation. But sweet friend, don't let rejection steal one more thing from you. Receive the little-known gifts of rejection that can work good in your life if you so choose. Here are three of those gifts I've embraced:

- **The gift of being made less.** When we decrease, God has room to make big things happen. We are reminded of this in John 3:28–31, as John the Baptist is insisting to his followers that he is "not the Anointed One; I am the one who comes before Him. . . . He, *the groom*, must take center stage; and I, *the best man*, must step to His side" (THE VOICE). Imagine what everyone would miss at a wedding if the best man refused to let the groom take his place. The radiant bride only walks down the aisle when she knows her groom is at the end ready to receive her. Then the glorious wedding happens.

  When writing on this passage, Eugene Peterson says, "That's why my cup is running over. This is the assigned moment for him to move into the center, while I slip off to the sidelines."[2] In this sideline, set-apart place, God will give you special wisdom you'll need for the next assignment. We'll take a look at this on a practical level in just a minute. But first, humility gifts two and three . . .

- **The gift of being lonely.** This will develop in you a deeper sense of compassion for your fellow travelers.

But in addition to the blessing of compassion being developed in me, those lonely times also seem to be when Jesus lavishes His most intimate compassion on me. Isn't it interesting that Jesus seemed to speak most intimately to people who were lonely? I doubt His conversation with the Samaritan woman at Jacob's Well in John 4 would have been the same if she'd been with a group of people. And we see a similar kind of personalized message for the woman caught in adultery in John 8. He didn't speak to her personally and intimately until the others left.

Both of these women were alone not just physically but emotionally and spiritually. We see them in extremely lonely and humbling situations. We see their aloneness. Then we see Jesus step into their loneliness and lavish His compassion on them, and, certainly with the Samaritan woman, a compassion for the others in her town emerged in her.

This is certainly what happens in my life as well. The conversations I have with the Lord in my loneliness always lead me to more intimacy with Him and more compassion for others. You better believe when I walk into a conference now, I look for someone sitting alone and make sure she knows she is noticed. When I ease the loneliness ache in others, it is beautifully eased in me.

- **The gift of silence.** Had I been surrounded by the voices of those people I was so eager to meet that night, I would surely have missed the voice of God. I'm trying to weave more silence into the rhythm of my life now, so I can whisper, "God, what might You want to say to me right now? I'm listening." Ecclesiastes tells us, "There is a time for everything, and a season for every activity under the heavens . . . a time to be silent and a time to speak" (3:1, 7).

I've got to spend time getting quiet so I can be prepared to hear new things from the Lord. Isn't it a lovely thought that God might be waiting for there to be silence in your life in order to share some of His best secrets with you? It was truly a profound secret from God's heart to mine when, in the silence, He whispered to my soul, *You are not set aside, you are set apart.* This statement settled me, changed me, and prepared me to share this same message with you.

I know it can painful to be alone. And I know the thoughts of being set aside are loud and overwhelmingly tempting to believe in the hollows of feeling unnoticed and uninvited. But as you pray through your feelings, see if maybe your situation has more to do with you being prepared than you being overlooked. There is something wonderfully sacred that happens when a girl chooses to realize that being set aside is actually God's call for her to be set apart.

Sometimes, though, when God calls us to be set apart for another purpose, it's difficult to believe God's goodness in

---

There is something wonderfully sacred that happens when a girl chooses to realize that being set aside is actually God's call for her to be set apart.

---

the hurt. Have you ever cried over something so much that you run out of tears? Your swollen eyes just give out and dry up while a current of unrest still gushes through your soul. And you look up toward heaven in utter frustration.

Me too.

And there's someone else in the Bible who was right there as well.

She felt provoked and irritated. Her anguish was so intense that she wept and would not eat. Before the Lord, she cried out in bitterness of soul, "LORD Almighty, if you will only look on your servant's misery and remember me, and not forget your servant . . . then I will . . ." (1 Samuel 1:11).

These words describe and articulate the deep distress of a woman from thousands of years ago, and yet here I sit in modern times and I relate so completely. They are from a woman named Hannah found in 1 Samuel 1. But you have to know that Hannah's expressions could have so easily come from me. Or even you.

Hannah's tears over her empty womb were made even more painful by her husband's other wife, Peninnah. She had many sons and daughters and made sure to rub this fact in Hannah's face every chance she got. In classic mean-girl style, Peninnah's actions targeted Hannah in her weakest place. "Because the LORD had closed Hannah's womb, her rival [Peninnah] kept provoking her in order to irritate her" (1:6).

There's a common thread that weaves through Hannah's story, and yours and mine. We all desperately want something that we see the Lord giving to other women. We see Him blessing them in the very areas He's withholding from us. And while these other women may not be obnoxious like Peninnah in their reminders of their blessing and our lack, it's increasingly painful each time we see a reminder. We look at them, and we feel set aside.

Why them? Why not me?

Then the seemingly unjust silence from God ushers us from a disturbed heart to weeping with bitterness of soul. And we start to feel something deep inside that comes in conflict with everything we hold true. *If God is good like we talked about in chapter 2, why isn't He being good to me* in this?

And in this moment of raw soul honesty, we're forced to admit we feel a bit suspicious of God. We've done all we know to do. We've prayed all we know to pray. We've stood on countless promises with a brave face. And still nothing.

Have you ever been suspicious of God in this way?

I'm not talking about wondering if God exists. This is not a struggle of intellectual debate peppered with facts. This is a struggle of emotional realities salted with feelings.

My head long ago nodded a big yes to His existence. It's because I know He exists and I know He loves me that things get so confusing and complicated. My heart struggles to make peace between God's ability to change hard things and His apparent decision not to change them for me.

In Hannah's case, we have the benefit of reading her story all the way through, and in a matter of four verses (17–20), her cries of anguish give way to the cries of her newborn son. But 1 Samuel 1:20 uses very clear words to let me know Hannah's answer didn't come right away: "So *in the course of time* Hannah became pregnant and gave birth to a son" (emphasis added).

And in the course of time, things will work out for me too. And things will work out for you. In the meantime, there's one more thing to add to the humility gifts we've already discussed: forgiving.

Standing in front of the mirror, thinking about thigh-gap girl, I tucked a strand of my hair behind my ear and swallowed hard, because I just didn't know what else to do. Instead of answers, all I kept hearing in response to my heart's cry were messages on forgiveness. Like unwelcome droplets of rain on a good hair day, I kept getting hit with quotes and songs and messages on forgiving.

Sadly, I felt like telling each one to go stick itself where the sun don't shine. Like in my lap region void of a thigh gap.

I know. I agree with you. That last admission is such evidence that awful had just eaten me up. From the top of my mind, entangled all about my heart, down to the tips of my toes, I resisted forgiving. Until I saw someone write the word this way: *For Giving.*

God made us For Giving.
God made you For Giving.
God made me For Giving.

And if we are for giving, we have to see opportunities taken away differently. What if this opportunity wasn't really taken away from me? What if I was actually spared of this gift, because for me it was really a burden in disguise?

What if my thigh-gap friend was actually doing me the greatest favor by fulfilling this assignment so I didn't have to? What if I was being set apart for something else? This is that special wisdom I mentioned in humility gift number one a few pages back. We won't think of this naturally. But if I choose to trust that this is God's protection for me and God's provision for her, it all lands in the good category.

In that, I can be all for giving this opportunity to her.

I can be all for giving God the trust He so absolutely deserves.

I can be all for giving myself space to back down, back away, and back off all the crazy emotions stealing my attention from the other gifts right in front of me today.

Instead of rejection, I can actually rejoice. This assignment wasn't meant for me. When I am for giving, I set us both up for winning.

She gets the assignment she was made to carry.

I'm freed up for other better-suited assignments tailor-made for me.

And neither of us gets caught in the wake of weird emotions stemming from me feeling rejected and bitter.

Of course, her toned thighs still trip me up a bit every now and then. But I'm doing this new exercise video that I ordered from the TV, which promises to lift and tuck and melt the flab away. I bet by the time we see each other in heaven, my legs are going to be looking oh-so-fine.

Or not.

Maybe my legs were built more for stability. No gentle breeze is gonna knock this girl over, that's for sure!

But no matter, because that's about the time Jesus will remind us that thighs aren't something we'll ever think about in eternity. And all God's girls say, "Hallelujah!"

Chapter 10

Her Success Does Not Threaten Mine

Several years ago, I remember pouring out all the best words I had in pixilated letters turned pages turned book proposal. I tucked my heart and dreams into a purple Office Max binder (because nothing says "I'm author material!" more than a purple Office Max binder) and hoped for the best.

That summer I gave my proposal to several acquisitions editors. I wanted the message I'd been working on to get into as many hands as possible, and I knew having a published book would accomplish this. These acquisitions editors held the key to making my dream come true.

For months after sending out my proposal, I would dream about the day some publishing house would say yes.

I can't tell you the number of afternoons I'd stand at my

mailbox, holding my breath and praying there would be good news inside. When the rejection letters started coming, I tried to keep up the hope that surely there would be one positive answer. I just needed one publisher to say yes.

Soon, I'd received a no answer from all but one. And when I got that final rejection, I felt so foolish for thinking I could actually write a book. My dream was nothing but a sham. I had no writing skills. And I must have heard God all wrong.

At the same time, I had wannabe writer friends who were getting different letters from the publishers.

Amazing letters.

Dreams-come-true letters.

Letters that turned into book contracts.

In my better moments, I did the right thing and authentically celebrated with them. But then there were other moments. Hard moments. Moments when I felt my friends' lives were rushing past me in a flurry of met goals, new opportunities, and affirmations of their callings from God. It seemed the world was literally passing me by.

In those moments I said, "Good for them." But on the inside I kept thinking, *Ouch . . . That means less and less opportunity for me.* The raw essence of honest hurting rarely produces pretty thoughts.

Why can't I see the kind of breakthrough she's experiencing?

She's so much better connected, resourced, and talented than me.

Since she's already successful with her endeavors, I wonder if there's even a need for mine.

When I wrote out these thoughts that had been running like a ticker tape in my mind, I was stunned at what I'd allowed. Not one of these statements was helpful. Not one of these statements was God-honoring. Not one of these statements acknowledged God's provision, which is big enough for us all.

Every one of these statements minimized God and maximized my weaknesses. That's not how we are supposed to think. We are supposed to maximize God, which keeps our weaknesses in perspective.

This was truly foolish thinking that stunk. And if we allow our thoughts to stink, that smell will leak out of every bit of us—our words, our actions, and especially our reactions. Proverbs 23:7 reminds us, "For as he thinks in his heart, so is he" (NLV). We've already unpacked a little bit of this back when we talked about the boxes of bitterness and grace, but because of how much it affects us, I think it's worth delving into a little deeper.

If we allow our thoughts to stink, that smell will leak out of every bit of us—our words, our actions, and especially our reactions.

The Stink

I have an adorable little three-pound dog named Willow. She's precious. She's sweet. I love to cuddle her. But there's one thing she does that I can't for the life of me understand. When she's freshly washed or freshly groomed, she will search our acreage for deer poop and roll in it until that horrid smell invades every inch of her. It truly is the strangest thing. And it does nothing to encourage me to want to bond with her. Nothing!

I love her, but when she rolls in that stink, it not only affects her; it affects me and everyone else in our home who comes close to her. Likewise, when you and I roll around in thoughts that stink, it affects the atmosphere everywhere we go. Stinking thoughts are not only unpleasant, they hint of death and not life.

As Jesus girls, we can't walk in victory while wallowing in thoughts of defeat and rejection. We must carry with us the sweet aroma of knowing Jesus everywhere we go. The apostle Paul wrote about this in 2 Corinthians 2:14: "But thanks be to God, who always leads us in triumph in Christ, and manifests through us the sweet aroma of the knowledge of Him in every place" (NASB).

When Paul wrote this, he had in his mind the procession that occurs with a Roman triumph:

> . . . the victorious general in his chariot with its white horses, the laurelled soldiers . . . the wreathing clouds of incense that went up into the blue sky, and the shouting multitude of spectators. . . . As the wreathing incense appealed at once to two senses, and was visible in its curling clouds of smoke, and likewise fragrant to the nostrils, so says Paul, with a singular combination of expression, "He maketh manifest," that is visible, the savour of His knowledge. From a heart kindled by the flame of the divine love there will go up the odor of a holy life visible and fragrant, sweet and fair.[1]

When we know Christ, it should show in our overflow, regardless of our relative success or discouragement in the face of rejection. From our hearts to our thoughts to our words to our actions, we have no business rolling in stink. As the commentary above stated: "From a heart kindled by the flame of the divine love there will go up the odor of a holy life visible and fragrant."

We are all prone to thoughts that stink. All of us. So, how do you stop the stink? I have yet to figure it out with my dog, Willow. But I have figured it out for you and me.

We must stop the scarcity thinking.

Scarcity Versus Abundance

What exactly is scarcity thinking? I like the way Stephen Covey put it in his book *7 Habits of Highly Effective People*:

> Most people are deeply scripted in what I call the Scarcity Mentality. They see life as having only so much, as though there were only one pie out there. And if someone were to get a big piece of the pie, it would mean less for everybody else.
>
> The Scarcity Mentality is the zero-sum paradigm of life. People with a Scarcity Mentality have a very difficult time sharing recognition and credit, power or profit—even with those who help in the production. They also have a very hard time being genuinely happy for the success of other people.
>
> The Abundance Mentality, on the other hand, flows out of a deep inner sense of personal worth and security.

It is the paradigm that there is plenty out there and enough to spare for everybody. It results in sharing of prestige, of recognition, of profits, of decision making. It opens possibilities, options, alternatives, and creativity.[2]

In other words, people who live with an abundance mentality, who operate out of a deep knowing of their immeasurable worth, live loved. Since Covey's book focuses mostly on dynamics in the business world, I wanted to know if the Bible ever specifically addressed an abundant approach to life versus one of scarcity.

And, boy, does it ever. As a matter of fact, it is woven into the very fabric of creation. Right from the beginning, God's way was an abundant way. Genesis 1 is all about God creating a good world blessed with abundant life potential tucked inside the DNA of every bit of His creation. His instruction to His creation was, "Be fruitful and multiply" (v. 28 THE VOICE).

The plants weren't limited. The animals weren't limited. People weren't limited. Inside each were seeds for more. This fruitful ability clearly speaks of God's goodness and abundance.

Psalm 104, the longest creation poem, is a commentary on Genesis 1. The Psalmist surveys creation and names it all; the heavens and the earth, the waters and springs and streams and trees and birds and goats and wine and oil and bread and people and lions. This goes on for 23 verses and ends in the 24th with the Psalmist's expression of awe and praise for God and God's creation. Verses 27 and 28 are something like a table prayer. They proclaim, "You give them all food in due season, you feed everybody." The Psalm makes clear that we don't need to worry. God is utterly, utterly reliable. The fruitfulness of the world is guaranteed.

Together, these scriptures proclaim that God's force of life is loose in the world. Genesis 1 affirms generosity and denies scarcity.

From Genesis 1 the pattern of abundance is lived out all the way until Genesis 47. Then things change in a dramatic way.

In that chapter Pharaoh dreams that there will be famine in the land. So Pharaoh gets organized to administer, control and monopolize the food supply. Pharaoh introduces the principle of scarcity into the world economy. For the first time in the Bible, someone says, "There's not enough. Let's get everything."

By the end of Genesis 47 Pharaoh has all the land except that belonging to the priests, which he never touches because he needs somebody to bless him. The notion of scarcity has been introduced into Biblical faith. The book of Exodus records the contest between the liturgy of generosity and the myth of scarcity—a contest that still tears us apart today.[3]

As I studied these scriptures, I really felt I was beginning to understand how this relates to my struggle with rejection.

If I look at my dreams, desires, and hopes for the future as coming from a place of scarcity and the world's limited supply, it will constantly feed the notion that someone else's success is a threat to mine. In other words, this person getting opportunities means less opportunity for me. Pharaoh, prompted by a dream drenched in fear, processed his worries through earthly thinking unguided by God. And suddenly other people having free access to food felt like a threat to him. That's not wisdom. That's fear. That's not how we are to process life.

We are to process life by looking up to the Lord and into His Word for wisdom. James 3:14–15 (ESV) says, "If you have bitter jealousy and selfish ambition in your hearts, do not boast and be false to the truth. This is not the wisdom that comes down from above, but is earthly, unspiritual, demonic."

What steals your heart away from God's wisdom? Might I take a tiny stab at what I think might have stolen at least a small part of you in the last hour? Social media.

Wait! Don't put the book down thinking I'm slamming social media. There are definitely good things happening there. But if it's stealing your heart away from God's wisdom, it's filling you with something else. This is something I know all too well.

It's easy to scroll and surf through postings—where people upload the beautiful, successful, shiny sides of life—and quickly get a jilted notion that maybe we're not quite keeping up. We feel small. Unnoticed. Incapable.

One day I realized I had to stop looking at things spotlighting others' successes until I had a better way of processing them. Until I could look at others and genuinely celebrate their lives without feeling anything but joy for them. I had to starve my scarcity thinking. How did I do this?

- *I started to ask Him to bless others and prayed this verse of abundance over them.*

   "And God is able to bless you abundantly, so that

in all things at all times, having all that you need, you will abound in every good work" (2 Corinthians 9:8).

- *I asked Him to help others succeed.*

   "Let each of you look not only to his own interests, but also to the interests of others" (Philippians 2:4 ESV).

- *I asked Him to send more people (not less) into ministry. We are all on the same team; therefore, I promised Him I would give them my knowledge and contacts.*

   This is what Jesus reminds us: "The harvest is great, but the workers are few. So pray to the Lord who is in charge of the harvest; ask him to send more workers into his fields" (Luke 10:2 NLT).

I knew I was finally getting somewhere when I could authentically say, "Her success does not threaten mine."

It's so true, sweet friend. When she does well, we all do well. All tides rise when we see a sister making this world a better place with her gifts. When I started believing this, my scarcity thinking started turning into abundance. And that was eighteen published books ago.

So even as the closed doors and rejections seem more prevalent than the new opportunities you'd like to see, even as you're seeking to readjust your thinking, remember that there is an abundant need in this world for your contributions to the kingdom . . . your thoughts and words and artistic expressions . . . your exact brand of beautiful.

Choose to live loved while you're in the middle of the journey, and know that what He has in mind for you is so much more than you imagine.

There is an

abundant

need in this

world for your

exact brand of

beautiful.

Chapter 11

❧

Ten Things You Must Remember When Rejected

I scooted into the restaurant booth beside my daughter Ashley. We ordered guacamole, extra ice for my unsweetened tea, and extra lemons for her water. She pulled out her phone and nervously tapped a few keys, then shoved it back into her purse. "I don't want to look yet."

Her first-semester college grades had been posted for two days, but she'd refused to look at them. We decided to do it together at one of our favorite restaurants. Together is a great way to press through something you're afraid could make you feel a bit undone.

She'd worked so hard. Her schedule had been incredibly challenging, and there'd been several sleepless nights when she wasn't sure she could push through. After all, school hasn't always been easy for Ashley. When she was in the eighth grade, her teachers requested a meeting with Art and me. We were stunned to find out that two months into that school year, she was failing every class.

It wasn't from her lack of effort. She'd turned in her assignments, and she'd studied for the tests. But she simply wasn't grasping the new curriculum her school had switched to that year. Her averages were so low that even if she started making As from that point on, things really couldn't be turned around. Their only suggestion was to have her go back and repeat seventh grade.

Immediately, I knew that would never work.

This school was a very small private school where it'd be really difficult to make a switch like this without hard questions, assumptions, and opinions. Middle school is not the time to proclaim to all your peers, "I can't cut it in eighth grade. So basically I'm going to hang with the seventh graders for the rest of this year."

I also think the school knew this wouldn't work. They offered to help us have her transferred to a different school.

It wasn't intended as a rejection. But it sure felt like one.

Sometimes what seems like a practical solution on one side can feel like a complete dissolution on the other. This private school that had once felt so right and so safe was now very much a closed door for our daughter. We had no choice but to transfer her to a public school where the kids would be oblivious to the fact that Ashley was repeating the seventh grade.

Her confidence was rocked. Her plans felt shaky. And her academic future seemed scary.

But two weeks into her fresh start at the new school, her

English teacher presented her with an award for a poem she'd written in class. This one boost of encouragement lit a spark in Ashley. Slowly, little successes at her new school gave her enough confidence to believe it was possible to turn things around. And by the end of that year, she was on the dean's list. By the time she got into high school, she was making great grades and even graduated with honors.

Now in college, she'd chosen an academically rigorous major. The freshman classes for that difficult major are known for weeding out many students. She was very aware of how challenging this would be.

She'd given it her all.

But the exams all carried a lot of weight toward her overall grades, and she just wasn't sure how she'd done. Now it was time to look at the results. I coaxed her to pull the phone back out and open the e-mail. Though that eighth-grade rejection was very far from her at that point, somehow the lingering fear from that past experience was as present at that lunch as the guacamole. This fear's ability to control her emotions was painfully obvious.

The enemy loves to take our rejection and twist it into a raw, irrational fear that God really doesn't have a good plan for us. This fear is a corrupting companion. It replaces the truths we've trusted with hopeless lies. Satan knows what consumes us controls us. Therefore the more consumed we are with rejection, the more he can control our emotions, our thinking, and our actions.

That's the exact place where panic starts to replace peace. Uncertainty starts to overshadow our faith. And discouragement threatens to override our joy.

What's a brokenhearted person to do? We must praise

God, seek God, look to God, call to God, experience God, fear God, learn from God, honor God, draw near to God, and take refuge in God.

This is how we take back control from something or someone that was never meant to have it and declare God as Lord. To help us see how we can practice this when the worries of rejection try to control us, here are ten things to remember and proclaim.

1. One Rejection Is Not a Projection of Future Failures

It's good to acknowledge the hurt, but don't see it as a permanent hindrance. Move on from the source of the rejection, and don't let it shut you down in that arena of life. It has already stolen enough from your present. Don't let it reach into your future.

No, that relationship didn't work out. But that doesn't mean you'll never find love. It also doesn't mean you aren't capable, likable, and lovely.

No, your book proposal wasn't a good fit for that publisher. But that doesn't mean you can't write. You don't have to have a published book to be an effective writer.

No, you didn't get that job opportunity. But that doesn't mean there won't be other interested companies.

No, Ashley didn't thrive at one school. But that didn't mean she couldn't thrive at another school.

Replace the negative talk that will hinder you. Replace it with praises for God, who will deliver you.

I will extol the LORD at all times;

    his praise will always be on my lips.

I will glory in the LORD;

    let the afflicted hear and rejoice.

Glorify the LORD with me;

    let us exalt his name together.

I sought the Lord, and he answered me;

    he delivered me from all my fears.

(PSALM 34:1–4)

2. Rejection Doesn't Label You; It Enables You to Adjust and Move On

It's our choice to have either a realistic view or a pessimistic view of rejection.

People with a realistic view see rejections as a natural part of life and adjust accordingly. It's not that they don't struggle through the hard feelings. They do. But they don't let them cloud their whole view of life. They are still able to see plenty of positive in themselves, others, and in God's plan.

Those with a pessimistic view, on the other hand, see life through the lens of their rejection. They feed their outlook by putting negative labels on themselves. When you feed negativity on the inside, it's negativity that you'll exude on the outside. This only compounds the hurt. Pessimists don't want to stay stuck in this downward spiral, but they feel swallowed up by the emotional shame of rejection.

You can only stop the spiral by replacing the labels.

Fill in the blank: This rejection doesn't mean I'm [whatever negative label or shame-filled feeling you are having]. It makes this [opportunity] [person] [desire] a wrong fit for me right now. Instead of letting the feelings from this situation label me, I'm going to focus on God and His promises for good things.

> Those who look to him are radiant;
>> their faces are never covered with shame.
>>
>> (PSALM 34:5)

3. This Could Be an Invitation to Live in Expectation of Something Else

Good things are coming. I know it. Today's disappointment is making room for tomorrow's appointment. Let's look for those good things with great intentionality.

Today's disappointment is making room for tomorrow's appointment.

I was reminded to do this by a friend I recently invited to go on a trip. She was thrilled and very much wanted to go. But as she prayed about it, she felt the Lord was telling her not to accept the invitation. She was confused, because she couldn't see one reason why this wasn't a good idea. But to be obedient to God, she texted me she would not be able to make the trip work.

I read her text and felt so bummed.

I wondered if her decline was for financial reasons or something else I could help her overcome. I picked up the phone and called her. She explained there weren't any specific reasons. She simply knew deep in her heart that God was saying this wasn't the way she was supposed to fill her schedule during that time period. Instead, she was to circle those days on her calendar and then watch with trust and expectation for God to reveal other plans.

I was so inspired by my friend's response. I want to live in expectation of God's invitation. Therefore, like my friend, I need to get better about looking for, recording, and focusing on these God appointments in the midst of disappointments.

Believing God has purposed our days will save us from the trouble of stepping into plans that aren't meant for us.

> I say to myself, "The LORD is my portion; therefore I will wait for him." The LORD is good to those whose hope is in him, to the one who seeks him; it is good to wait quietly for the salvation of the LORD. (Lamentations 3:24–26)

4. There Is Usually Some Element of Protection Wrapped in Every Rejection

This is a hard one to process at the time of the rejection. But for many of my past rejections, I can look back and see how God was allowing things to unfold the way they did for my protection.

In His mercy, He allowed this.

It was a mercy ruin. It's easy for us to focus on the ruin. But look for His mercy in the midst of it. In the mercy we'll find the protection. In the mercy you can see things falling into place rather than falling apart. I see this in what appeared to be the ruin of Ashley needing to switch schools. I'm not sure we would have made such a move had the school not forced our hand. Our other kids were thriving there and needed to stay. Having Ashley at a different school added some complexities we wouldn't have wanted to take on. But we had no other choice.

I didn't realize how much Ashley needed this change. But the Lord certainly knew what He was doing when He allowed all this to unfold. All the wonderful tenacity tucked inside Ashley was being slowly stripped out of her in an environment where she felt she couldn't ever get ahead. Switching to a different school gave her a chance to start over.

When I see her thriving now, I see the protection in this. I no longer think of that other school in terms of holding Ashley back. I now see they helped us set her free. This helps me trust God's protection in other rejection situations where I can't see it. Maybe you are in one of those situations right now . . .

When that wonderful, godly man walks away, where's the protection in that?

When that opportunity didn't come through that would have helped so much financially, where's the protection in that?

When several close friends go on a girl's weekend and neglect to include you, where's the protection in that?

Into that space of not understanding, we simply must state, "God, I don't understand this situation. But I do understand Your goodness to me. I thank You for the protection that is part of this rejection even when I can't see it. I trust You."

The angel of the LORD encamps around those who fear him,
> and he delivers them.

Taste and see that the LORD is good;
> blessed is the one who takes refuge in him.
Fear the LORD, you his holy people,
> for those who fear him lack nothing.
The lions may grow weak and hungry,
> but those who seek the LORD lack no good thing.

(PSALM 34:7–10)

5. It's Good to Ask the "What" Questions but Less Helpful to Ask "Why"

Decide you'll only ask questions that help you move forward instead of feeling stuck in the reasons something happened. "What" questions increase our ability to become more self-aware, while "why" questions only focus on things out of our control.

Pride loves to whisper, "It's their issue. Not yours." Insecurity loves to whisper, "You are a mess. You are the issue." But what a tragedy it would be to suffer this hurt and refuse the precious and costly gifts of humility and maturity this situation could very well give you.

Questions I've found helpful:

- What is one good thing I've learned from this?
- What was a downside to this situation that I can be thankful is no longer my burden to carry?
- What were the unrealistic expectations I had, and how can I better manage these next time?

- What do I need to do to boost my courage to pursue future opportunities?
- What is one positive change I could make in my attitude about the future?
- What are some lingering negative feelings about this situation that I need to pray through and shake off to be better prepared to move forward?
- What is one thing God has been asking me to do today to make tomorrow easier?

I've also found it helpful to write these things down. And get some solid friends around you to help you think through these questions. Chances are they can help you see things you'll miss on your own. The Lord is wooing us to listen and learn these lessons that will help us look more and more like Him.

> Come my children, listen to me;
> I will teach you the fear of the LORD.
>
> (PSALM 34:11)

6. Don't Hash, Bash, or Trash on the Internet. Remember, the Internet Never Forgets.

It's good to have a trusted and wise friend to process rejection with. She will be able to let your emotions work themselves out without forever labeling you as irrational. The World Wide Web and social media, on the other hand, won't be so forgiving.

Wisdom makes decisions today that will still be good for tomorrow. Don't let today's reaction become tomorrow's regret. Even using the seemingly innocent emojis that hint at broken hearts, crying rivers of tears, and stunned confusion will only invite the public into your very private need to heal.

If you feel that you need more intensive help, find a Christian counselor to meet with. It doesn't mean you are unhealthy or

---

Don't let today's reaction become
tomorrow's regret.

---

unstable if you see a counselor. Actually, some of the most well-adjusted people I know attribute their healthy ways of processing emotions to the counselors they've seen through-out the years.

> Whoever of you loves life
>   and desires to see many good days,
> keep your tongue from evil
>   and your lips from telling lies.
>
> (PSALM 34:12–13)

7. There's Much More to You than the Part That Was Rejected

One of the hard parts of rejection is the time gap it suddenly introduces into your life. Chances are you're used to a routine that included set-aside time for the person or opportunity that rejection has taken from you. Now that the pursuit has ended, it's so easy to feel completely lost.

Use this extra time to discover new things about yourself.

That's how I discovered my passion for writing. I'd tried and failed at several creative pursuits when I first quit my full-time job to stay home with the kids.

And when I say failed, we're talking went down in flames! The list included:

- **Floral designer.** I was allergic to something in the shop, and my constant struggle with this annoyed the shop owner to no end. Eventually, she said she wanted to free me to pursue other endeavors . . . aka . . . you're fired.
- **Wedding planner.** I threw up at the very first wedding I helped plan. And not quietly in the bathroom by myself. Nope. I'll just let your imagination fill in the gaps from here.
- **Mural painter.** It's an amazing endeavor to want to paint. But when you can't paint . . . it's problematic.
- **Kitchen tools seller.** When you are telling a roomful of potential customers how safe your gadget is and simultaneously slice off the end of your finger, it's both gross and career ending.

(Please forgive me if you were a client at one of these said failed endeavors!)

It was such a bumpy ride. But tucked inside each of these failed endeavors were clues that I was made to create. But my assignment wasn't floral arrangements or wedding experiences or paintings or cuisine; it was stringing words together through writing. Had I been successful at those other jobs, I may never have pursued my real calling.

I no longer look at those things as career-defining failures.

I now see them as clues pointing in a better direction—the right direction for me.

You are more than you know, my friend. So much more.

> The LORD makes firm the steps
>> of the one who delights in him;
> though he may stumble, he will not fall,
>> for the LORD upholds him with his hand.
>
> (PSALM 37:23–24)

8. What One Person Sees as Your Liability, Another Might See as a Wonderful Asset

The other day I posted something on social media about a harsh letter I received years ago. The purpose of the post wasn't to wallow in the past but rather to help others going through this same kind of rejection process their hurt with hope.

Many women thanked me and found the post to be very helpful, hopeful, and encouraging. But one gal saw this post as proof that I wasn't walking in freedom and felt the need to challenge me. The first time I read her comment, I thought, *What in the world?!*

But then I realized it was my vulnerability she didn't like. What many saw as an asset of mine, she saw as a liability. A good question to ask myself in this situation is, "While this quality is good to most, am I using it in its most mature form?"

This commenter didn't think a Bible teacher should display her feelings. To her, this was a sign of weakness. And, to be honest, in the absence of maturity, this could absolutely be a detriment in ministry. It's not bad that I'm vulnerable, but am I displaying a mature form of my vulnerability? This is a really good thing to consider instead of just blowing off her comment.

I have to remember that her opinion is not the whole truth. While it's good to consider what she said, I must make the choice not to get consumed by it. I have to keep it all in perspective.

God's eyes are on me. His face is not against me. And even if others appear to be against me, I must make sure in my reaction to them that I extend grace and honor God.

> "Love your enemies, do good to those who hate you, bless those who curse you, pray for those who mistreat you."
> (Luke 6:27–28 NASB)

9. This Is a Short-Term Setback, Not a Permanent Condition

The emotions that feel so intense today will ease up over time as long as we let them. We just have to watch how we think and talk about this rejection. If we give it the power to define us, it will haunt us long-term. But if we only allow it enough power to refine us, the hurt will give way to healing.

Remember that guy I mentioned in chapter 7 who I was convinced was my future husband? When he broke up with me, the pain was so intense that for months I would find myself grabbing my chest, wondering if I was having a heart attack.

I replayed and relived our breakup hundreds of times and felt life sort of stopped for me that tear-filled night. That rejection tried to take up permanent residence in my heart with the statement, "I'm never going to get over this." Months later, I was challenged to stop saying those words and stop believing this was a permanent condition forever defining my life.

I took that challenge seriously and got rid of every reminder of him. Reminders of him were triggers for me. I took down all his pictures from my room. I threw away his love letters and cards. And I gave away a necklace he'd given me. There was no social media back then, but in today's terms that would have meant unfollowing him. That may seem extreme, but I had to have a complete break if I was going to completely heal.

Slowly my emotions stopped feeling controlled by that heartbreak.

Eventually, I got to the place where I learned from my mistakes in that relationship and moved on as a refined person. Then other relationships could breathe life back into that wounded and wilted place of my heart.

Though it felt so permanent at the time, in the scope of my life, I can now see it was truly just a short-term setback from which the Lord delivered me.

> The righteous cry out, and the Lord hears them;
> he delivers them from all their troubles.
>
> (Psalm 34:17)

10. Don't Let This Heartbreak Destroy You. Let This Breaking Actually Be the Making of You. Let God Use It in Good Ways to Make You Stronger and Take You Further.

There's a line from the prayer that Art's dad prayed over us at our wedding that I think of quite often: "Lord, give them enough hurts to keep them human and enough failures to keep their hands clenched tightly in Yours."

There were many other lines of blessing in the prayer, but this part made me tilt my head, heavy with about fifty-two pounds of sprayed-up curls and a homemade veil. Praying for hurts and failures in the wedding ceremony? My face flushed at the realization I'd forgotten to cross that part out.

I'd seen the prayer beforehand. It was all typed out. But in the rush of everything, I'd forgotten. And now, we had essentially asked God for heartbreak. At our wedding. Awesome.

But Art's dad is a wise man. And I'm thankful he didn't take it upon himself to strike that part. I couldn't have understood the prayer on that day full of white tulle, giddy whispers of love, and my three-year-old sister singing "Happy Birthday" during the lighting of the unity candle. But as life has unfolded, I now very much understand the beauty of those lines.

Our life could have been very self-focused. Our marriage. Our home. Our kids. Our plans. Our life.

But God wanted so much more from us. He didn't bring us together simply to build a life that would make us happy. He brought us together to be partners in the purpose He assigned. Our own strength would not have prepared us for kingdom assignments. It would have crippled us. The breaking of us has actually been the making of us . . . the God-strengthened us He could use.

Heartbreak is a part of life. It's certainly been a part of different seasons of my marriage. And though every single hurt seemed like an exposure of weakness in our relationship, it actually brought out a strength we couldn't have gotten any other way.

And for those of you whose marriage didn't remain standing under the weight of life, please don't get stuck thinking these truths are only for couples. Do not let the heartbreak you have experienced be wasted. God is still with you. His promises still stand. Soak in His truths and let them seep into the deepest places of your heart rubbed raw with uncertainty.

Married or not, don't let what breaks your heart destroy your life.

Hold fast to Jesus and remember: This breaking of you will be the making of you. A new you. A stronger you. Strengthened not with the pride of perfection but with the sweet grace of one who knows an intimate closeness with her Lord.

> The LORD is close to the brokenhearted
> and saves those who are crushed in spirit.
>
> (PSALM 34:18)

Using the original language for this verse, you could read it like this: *The Lord draws near to the one who has had her heart shattered and delivers her from exposed grief to victory.*

He draws you near despite the sharp evidence of your grieving heart. The anger. The deep disappointment and disillusionment. The questions of why you and why now? The comparisons that make you feel as though God loves other people more. How could He let this happen? The cussing and banging your fist on the steering wheel. The shame and anguish. All of these are shards of being shattered.

God isn't afraid of your sharp edges that may seem quite risky to others. He doesn't pull back. He pulls you close. His love and grace covers your exposed grief. And step-by-step

God isn't *afraid*
of your *sharp* edges

that may seem

quite *risky* to others.

He doesn't pull back.

He pulls you *close*.

leads you to a new place of victory. A sweet place your soul is so glad to be in though you never would have chosen the hard path on your own.

Back to Ashley at the restaurant, letting the past school rejection taunt her. Remember: what consumes us, controls us. As I helped her process her fears through the filter of truth, courage emerged that no matter what—good or bad— she could trust God.

And please understand: I didn't preach a sermon to her. It only took a few reminders of truth to see more clearly. Lies flee in the presence of truth.

Finally, she clicked open the e-mail revealing her grades. Not only did she pass; she was on the dean's list.

I was so thankful that day hers were tears of joy. But I'm also well aware that in the tomorrows that come, things could be different. Rejections big and small just seem to ebb and flow in and out of life. Troubles will probably still find us. But the Lord doesn't just deliver us from *some* of our troubles. Psalm 34:19–20 tells us He delivers us from them *all*!

> The righteous person may have many troubles,
>> but the LORD delivers him from them all;
> he protects all his bones,
>> not one of them will be broken.

And I'll give that truth a big, huge AMEN!

Chapter 12

The Enemy's Plan Against You

I'm not a fan of lions. Not. At. All. Because they aren't picky with their food choices. Whether you're a gazelle that got separated from your herd or a tourist crazy enough to sleep in a tent where lions roam, they'll think you look amazing. And it really makes no difference to them if you're covered in animal fur or a Gap T-shirt. They will stalk you if they're hungry.

These creatures have woven into their DNA an animal instinct that's nearly impossible to override. You can try to train them. You can try to domesticate them. And for a while you might even be able to snuggle them like a pet. But coursing underneath their tamed appearance is the instinct of a wild, wild beast.

A beast I never thought I'd encounter face-to-face.

But I was wrong.

When my family and I decided we wanted to go back to

the continent where my two sons were born and do missions work, a splinter of fear shot through my heart. But then I scolded myself for being so stereotypical. White girl in America thinks of Africa and instantly sees huts and lions. Shame on me.

I tossed my fear aside as I packed a ridiculous amount of clothes and hair products to head to the mission field. We were off to save the world. Or at least feed some beautiful kids in an orphanage tucked at the base of Mount Kilimanjaro in Tanzania.

We loved and we learned and we left with a lump of emotion in our throats. And then we made good on the promise to our family that we'd go on an African picture-taking safari our last two nights there. We pulled up to our accommodations, and I swallowed hard. Partly because the dust from the drive covered every inch of me and coated my throat with the unpleasant feeling I'd been snacking on sand.

But also because I saw tents.

For real. They were fabric sided and triangular shaped, with zipper closures for front doors.

In the spirit of full disclosure, let me add that they were sitting on top of wooden platforms, and each had a bed and a potty inside. This was a good thing considering there was a large sign strongly encouraging us not to ever leave our tents after dark—for any reason. An indoor potty was a total bonus for my forty-year-old bladder that acts like a newborn in its refusal to sleep through the night. It's a situation I share with you because by this time in the book, I totally consider you a friend, and friends share this kind of stuff.

But back to that sign. About not leaving your tent after dark. Ever.

There was another small detail on this sign you should know about: the instruction not to keep any food in the tent. We're talking not a cracker or even the ten little M&Ms that sit at the bottom of your purse in case of a really desperate day.

I quickly discerned the opposition to us having snacks wasn't some sort of effort to help us manage our weight. It was because the lions would smell the food and come after it. And in the process come after us.

Call me loopy, but I was suddenly no longer in the mood to be in a tent in Africa with snack-crazy lions nearby.

My people, on the other hand, find situations like this thrilling. They jump off rock quarries, swim with sharks, and wish they could be tornado chasers. I much prefer to sit in a quiet corner, reading books and eating emergency M&Ms for a thrill.

To say I was fretting nightfall is quite an understatement.

Art announced he was going to bed and, just like that, drifted into a cozy little dream. Meanwhile, I had a death grip on the top of the bedsheet and could hear my heart drumming against the lumpy mattress. I wanted to take a sleeping pill, but when I found the empty wrapper, it confirmed a terrible thing. Art had already taken one. This meant that I was the only one sober enough to ward the lions away should they venture into camp, albeit armed with nothing but sheer terror and absolute anxiety.

The guides had assured us the lions wouldn't come.

They lied.

Right when I was flirting with the edges of sleep, a creature brushed the length of my tent and—wait for it—roared!

Think of the sound that monster under your bed from your childhood imagination would undoubtedly make whenever he jumped out to get you. Now magnify that by about ten times, African animal-style.

And then the lion moaned and whined as he brushed the tent again, this time inches from my head.

Art, the calm one who fixes stuff like this, had been rendered useless by his night-night pill. I was infuriated the sign hadn't instructed all husbands against taking sleeping medicine.

I held my body perfectly still, barely letting air in and out of my lungs. But my mind wouldn't cooperate. It fired off one imagined scene after another of all the worst scenarios and horrific outcomes that could possibly come of this rather unfortunate situation.

Though I never stepped outside the tent or touched a beast of any sort, I suffered a brutal attack of the mind. I wrestled that lion. And lost. Because I let him get the best of my thoughts.

I'm not writing about this scenario so that you'll be better prepared if you're ever on safari, staying in a tent. You don't have to go to Africa to get stalked by a lion.

There's a roaring lion waiting just around every next thought you think. And make no mistake: there's no taming him. He's a defeated foe who has already suffered a fatal blow. But before he falls, he'll try to make a few last kills. With everything he's got left, he's coming after your mind.

This injured lion is the most vicious of all. "Your enemy the devil prowls around like a roaring lion looking for someone to devour" (1 Peter 5:8).

He's not just looking to distract you, or tempt you, or pull you slightly off course. He's looking to *devour* you. But we must remember something crucial. The Devil is vicious, but he's not victorious. And you, my friend, have everything you need to defeat him. You don't have to lie there shaking in your bed with a death grip on the covers, feeling powerless and deathly afraid.

The Devil is powerful, but he's also predictable. We are told in 1 John 2:16 the exact three ways he's going to come after us. "For everything in the world—the cravings of sinful man, the lust of his eyes and the boasting of what he has and does—comes not from the Father, but from the world."

He's coming after me today by making me want to get my needs met outside the will of God. He will dangle scenarios in front of me that evoke feelings that tempt me to crave, lust, and boast.

- **Crave:** I feel empty.

    Whenever I feel lonely or less than, I think I can fill my emptiness with temporary physical pleasures. The things I consume soon consume my thoughts. What started as a little thing has become something of which I can't ever quite get enough.
- **Lust:** I feel deprived.

    When my eyes see the shiny, sexy, and slick things others have, I can become laser focused that I need something to make my life more shiny. Justifications come easy. Rationalizations numb my conscience. Be it a possession, person, or position, I'm lured by the intoxicating notion that I can sneak outside the will of God to get what I want and it's no big deal.
- **Boast:** I feel rejected.

    Do I ever post something on social media to try and make myself feel better or more accepted? The

The Devil is

vicious,

but he's not

victorious.

likes and comments ward off the stings of rejection but at what cost? Is it just a masked form of boasting when I pick the picture that makes my life appear a little more polished than it actually is?

The Devil wants me to fill my emptiness with an unhealthy dependence on the acceptance of others. Because then he can get me so focused on the shallow opinions of others I get completely distracted from deepening my relationship with Christ. And in the process is my masked boasting pulling others into the crazy comparison traps that lures them away from Christ as well? It's all such an unhealthy cycle that's never satisfying. And again, I'm not against social media but we do have to be so careful how we use it. Is it to bless others with encouragement and love or are we really just boasting on ourselves and feeding others' unhealthy comparisons to us? One quick hop on social media, and you'll see how careful we must be not to play right into the Devil's schemes.

According to a 2015 study I conducted in partnership with Barna Group, women ages eighteen and older in the United States go to social media looking to connect and feel better about themselves, but only 14 percent walk away feeling encouraged. That's a whopping 86 percent who may be going about their day feeling emptier and more deprived than before.

Nearly half of women report feeling lonely at least occasionally after spending time on social media. Sixty-two percent of Millennials say they feel lonely at least occasionally, with one in ten saying they *usually* do.[1]

It's also interesting to me that six out of ten women say they feel like they want to change something about their lives at least occasionally after looking at social media. More than

78 percent of Millennials feel that way at least occasionally, with 21 percent saying they *usually* do.

I understand it's hard to put a face to a statistic. So I decided to ask my Facebook friends how they would describe their experiences with social media to see if it lined up with the research.

And it did.

Donna N. said, "I'm connected to so many, yet I feel lonelier. Isn't anyone out there having a bad day, too? Life feels less honest somehow."

Kelly S. said, "I can't help but compare myself to others' lives and feel like I don't measure up. People are only posting the positive stuff, so it's easy to look at it and feel like they don't have their own problems."

Shelbie B. said, "I feel lonely and left out. It's not right when I see women from my church posting pictures of themselves out having a good time and I have not been invited. I feel lonely all the time as I do try to make friends but everyone seems so disconnected. If I could just have one close friend it would mean so much to me."

My heart aches when I read these brutally honest confessions.

Again, I'm not against social media being used in healthy ways. But we sure do need to be honest with ourselves. Is it helping us fight the lion, or is it actually feeding it?

And when I said the Devil is predictable, he totally is. These are the same three ways he tempted Jesus in Matthew 4:1–11.

After Jesus had fasted for forty days, the Devil placed stones in front of Him, knowing Jesus could easily turn them into bread. Bread that could fill His emptiness.

Jesus knew what empty felt like.

The Devil also showed Him worldly wealth and splendor.

Jesus had emerged from a stable and hardly progressed past the basics of belongings. Having lived in perfection with memories of heaven, He found that every one of His earthly realities fell short.

Jesus knew what being deprived felt like.

The Devil also reminded Jesus of an untapped power source that would have surely silenced the skeptics and corrected the critics. Those who shunned Him and shamed Him would suddenly bow down before Him. Can you imagine the restraint it surely took not to throw Himself down and, in a sweep of angelic majesty, be elevated and worshipped by heavenly beings?

Jesus knew what being rejected felt like.

Jesus knew. He knew the feelings. He knew the struggles. And in an earth-shattering moment, Jesus exposed the way of escape for us. He matched every feeling—the emptiness, the deprivation, and the rejection—with truths straight from God's Word.

Lies flee in the presence of truth.

Lies flee in the presence of truth.

And the Devil turns powerless when our minds turn to our all-powerful God.

Here's where I become quite fascinated. Jesus had access to thousands of scriptures from the Old Testament. He knew them. He could have used any of them. But He chose three specific ones. I've decided I want these three to be at the top of my mind.

I Want a Promise for My Problem of Feeling Empty

Man does not live on bread alone but on every word that comes from the mouth of the LORD. (Deuteronomy 8:3)

My soul was hand designed to be richly satisfied in deep places by the Word of God. When I go without the nourishment of truth, I will crave filling my spiritual hunger with temporary physical pleasures, thinking they will somehow treat the loneliness inside. These physical pleasures can't fill me, but they can numb me. Numb souls are never growing souls. They wake up one day feeling so very distant from God and wondering how in the world they got there.

Since Satan's goal is to separate us from the Lord, this is exactly where he wants us to stay. But the minute we turn to His Word is the minute the gap between us and God is closed. He is always near. His Word is full and fully able to reach those deep places inside us desperate for truth.

I Want a Promise for My Problem of Feeling Deprived

"Fear the LORD your God, serve him only and take your oaths in his name" (Deuteronomy 6:13). Another version of this verse says, "Worship Him, your True God, and serve Him." (THE VOICE)

When we worship God, we reverence Him above all else. A great question to ask: *Is my attention being held by something sacred or something secret?* What is holding my attention the most is what I'm truly worshipping.

Sacred worship is all about God.

Is my attention being held by something sacred or something secret?

Secret worship is all about something in this world that seems so attractive on the outside but will devour you on the inside.

Pornography, sex outside of marriage, trading your character to claw your way to a position of power, fueling your sense of worth with your child's successes, and spending outside of your means to constantly dress your life in the next new thing—all things we do to counteract feelings of being left out of and not invited to the good things God has given others—these are just some of the ways lust sneaks in and wreaks havoc. Two words that characterize misplaced worship or lust are *secret excess*.

God says if we will direct our worship to Him, He will give us strength to turn from the mistakes of yesterday and provide portions for our needs of today.

> Whom have I in heaven but you?
>   And earth has nothing I desire besides you.
> My flesh and my heart may fail,
>   but God is the strength of my heart
>   and my portion forever.
>
> (PSALM 73:25–26)

And I Certainly Want a Promise for My Problem of Feeling Rejected

Do not put the LORD your God to the test. (Deuteronomy 6:16)

At first glance I don't understand why Jesus chose Deuteronomy 6:16 to combat rejection. And it almost makes me doubt this third part has anything to do with it. But then it stirs my heart so wonderfully when I tuck it back in the context of the other verses around it. Verses 13–15 remind us, "Fear the LORD your God, serve him only and take your oaths in his name. Do not follow other gods, the gods of the peoples around you; for the LORD your God, who is among you, is a jealous God."

He is jealous for you. He is jealous for me. The fullness of His love and lavish acceptance is the only match for the rejections we will experience. And He absolutely doesn't want us making other relationships the false gods of our worship. As we seek love and acceptance, God doesn't want us to test Him; He wants us to trust Him.

When He says we are holy and dearly loved children, we must trust that this is true.

Studying these three promises proclaimed by Jesus has captured my heart. When I remember the promises of God, I tap into the power of God. God's promises are always a perfect match for our problems. And our problem instigator the Devil—the lion—is no match for God's promises.

Promises don't tame the lion; they shame the lion back to hell. They shut his mouth. Turn his roar into a whimper. And make him run timid when the Bible-toting, Scripture-memorizing girl in the Gap T-shirt looks his way. She is terrifyingly brave and so very beautiful.

That's you.

That's me.

We just have to remember that where we pay attention matters more than we know. Our minds and hearts are like dry sponges. What we focus on is what will soak in and saturate us. If it is something foolish, we will make foolish decisions. If it is wise, we will make wise decisions.

Satan knows this. So he constantly puts things in front of us to try and grab our attention. Remember: like a lion is drawn to a food source, Satan rushes in where he smells emptiness, deprivation, and rejection.

If we pay attention to foolish things or things that fuel foolishness in us, we will bankrupt our perspective. And we will be more likely to fall prey to Satan's schemes. Satan's schemes are well-thought-through plans specifically targeted at our particular weakness to do three things:

- To increase our desire for something outside the will of God
- To make us think giving in to a weakness is no big deal
- To minimize our ability to think through the consequences of falling to this temptation

Can I take your hand right now and look you straight in the eyes with a pleading statement? You are more susceptible to Satan's schemes when you are feeling rejected. Emotional pain will scream for relief, and it's so easy to start justifying thoughts and actions outside God's will.

That's why it's crucial to watch what is influencing me and

feeding my thoughts. A good question to ask myself is, where am I paying my attention?

Specifically, what am I paying attention to first thing in the morning? And what am I paying attention to right before I go to sleep? If I want God to be my focus, I must give Him my first thoughts. And if I want my mind to be at peace when I sleep I must keep my thoughts fixed on His promises at night . . . whether I'm in a tent on the African plain or not.

Obviously, I don't have lions regularly brush by my house, but I don't want to forget that night in the tent when I experienced the reality of the prowl, the roar, the danger. It was frightening. But the lion's power over me stopped the minute the guards showed up with tranquilizer guns. One shot and the lion fell.

Truth is the perfect tranquilizer. The enemy's power is rendered powerless in the presence of God's promises.

Remember this. Receive this. Use this. Practice this. Live this.

Chapter 13

∽

Miracles in the Mess

I ran my hand over the large rock and closed my eyes. What an incredible moment it was for me to stand where Jesus once stood. I opened my Bible and let the full reality of all He faced when He stood in this same place fall fresh on me.

I wanted to read the scriptures leading up to this moment when He sat on Mount Arbel and prayed and watched the disciples just before He walked on water. I cautioned myself to note the uncommon sentences. Too many times I highlight verses telling of Jesus' miracles but skim right past those telling of deeply human realities.

In Mark 5, for example, we see Jesus interacting with a woman desperate to be healed from her bleeding disorder. He frees her from her suffering and gives her peace. We also find Him healing the young daughter of a synagogue ruler.

Miracles!

But then there's verse 40: "They laughed at him."

In Mark 6 we find Jesus sending out the twelve disciples, and as they preached, "they drove out many demons and anointed many sick people with oil and healed them" (v. 13).

Miracles!

But we also find verse 3: "And they took offense at him."

We see Him having great compassion on the people who followed Him in the feeding of the five thousand. They all ate and were satisfied by five loaves and two fish.

Miracle!

But we also see that Jesus and His disciples were physically depleted "because so many people were coming and going that they did not even have a chance to eat" (v. 31).

Messy realities in the midst of the miracles.

And isn't it so like us to miss this about Jesus' everyday life? We hyper-focus on the lines of Scripture containing the miracles, and we miss the details of the mess.

People laughed at Jesus. People rejected Jesus. People misunderstood Jesus. We know this in theory, but as I sat on that rock that day, I suddenly realized what an everyday reality this was for Him. And because this was a reality for Him, He is the perfect one to turn to when rejection is a reality for us.

He understands. He teaches us from that tender place of knowing this pain personally. And, best of all, He chose to do His miracles in the midst of messy realities. Remember this. Don't get so consumed by and focused on the mess—the feelings of rejection, hurt, and disillusionment—that you miss the miracle.

That's the very thing that happened to the disciples right after the feeding of the five thousand. They got in a boat and quickly found themselves in rough waters, tossed by strong winds. They strained at the oars as the realities of life beat against them.

This storm was a terrifying mess for them. The waves weren't just ebbing, cresting, and crashing like you've probably seen if you've ever been in rough waters. These waves were bubbling up and exploding all around them in unpredictable ways. Think what it looks like when you place a straw in a glass of water and blow with great force. They couldn't brace themselves or their boat. They were completely helpless.

Jesus was on the mountainside praying. And from this spot he could see the middle of the lake. Mark 6:47–48 says, "Later that night, the boat was in the middle of the lake, and he was alone on land. He saw the disciples straining at the oars, because the wind was against them."

Jesus saw them. He went down to them. And they missed the miracle in the midst of the mess. The same miracle worker they had watched multiply the fish and the loaves was now walking on the water near them. And they thought He was a ghost:

> They cried out, because they all saw him and were terrified.
> Immediately he spoke to them and said, "Take courage! It is I. Don't be afraid." Then he climbed into the boat with them, and the wind died down. They were completely amazed, for they had not understood about the loaves; their hearts were hardened. (vv. 49–52)

The word *hardened*, as it is used here, means "unresponsive, completely lacking sensitivity or spiritual perception."

How can this be? How could it possibly be that the disciples' hearts were lacking sensitivity and spiritual perception? They had been with Jesus! The fullness of God had breathed on them, walked with them, served alongside them, and worked miracles in the midst of them.

I can tell you how. They had witnessed expressions of God, but they hadn't turned those expressions into personal experiences. The NASB translation of verse 52 hints at this: "for they had not gained any insight from the incident of the loaves, but their heart was hardened."

The Greek word for *insight* here is syníēmi, which means to put facts together to arrive at an understanding complete with life applications. The disciples had not done that with the miracle of the loaves and fishes.

In other words, they had seen a lot. They had heard a lot. But they had not personally applied what they'd seen and heard. Their hearts were not tender to the reality of Jesus. Their hearts were hardened. Access without application will not equal transformation.

How does this relate to us?

We can go to Bible study and amen every point made, but if we don't apply it to our lives, we won't be changed. And I'll even take it a step further and say that if we've been exposed to a teaching that we know we need to implement and we don't make any changes, that's a clue that the hardening of that part of our heart is in process.

Inspiration and information without personal application will never amount to transformation.

A rock song can inspire us. The nightly news can inform us. But it is only by applying the truth of God to our lives that we can be transformed in the direction of God's best for us. Romans 12:2 reminds us to be "transformed" by the renewing of our minds. It's that shift in thinking we've been talking

Inspiration

and *information*

without personal

application

will never amount to

transformation.

about, operating out of fullness and living loved despite whatever circumstances may be surrounding us.

The disciples were surely inspired by Jesus' miracle. And they were certainly informed by His teaching. But because they had not personally applied what they learned, they weren't transformed.

Only when we seek to apply His revelations to our situations will we experience transformation. Transformation helps us more clearly see Jesus. And when we more clearly see Him, we can more clearly see the miracle in our mess, the good in our difficulty, the redemption in rejection.

How tragic that Jesus miraculously walked on water to come save His disciples in the middle of the mess of this storm, and they didn't recognize Him.

They were close to Him but unaware of His presence. They could hear Him but could not grasp His promises. And they surely needed Him but did not take hold of His provision.

And they were terrified.

Please, please, please don't miss this. Any place where we have hardened our hearts or refused to let truth touch and transform that part of us, there will be confusion. Just like the disciples seeing Jesus walking toward them and thinking He was a ghost.

What did they do in the midst of this confusion? They cried out in fear instead of calling out to their Lord in faith. They were terrified. Why? Let's look at that word *terrified* as it is used in these scriptures. It's *tarasso*, which means "to set in motion what needs to remain still."

Can we all just sit down and soak in this little gem for a half a minute . . . or actually for forever?

The miracle in the midst of their mess was walking toward

them. The One who could speak to the water. Calm the waves. Hush the storm. The One who loved them and would give His very life to save them. The One who had complete compassion and deep devotion to protect them.

But they missed Jesus . . . so they set in motion what needed to remain still. They were terrified. They were anxious. They were desperate. All that was set in motion.

Do you know how much drama and heartbreak I could have avoided in my life if I would not have set into motion what needs to remain still? Every time this has happened in my life, I can draw a straight line to decisions I made from a hardened heart. The disciples had their own issues that led to their hearts becoming hardened, but what is it that has so often led me to this condition? Trading God's truth for what the world said was a better plan.

Resisting God's promises will make us forget God's presence.

Resisting God's promises will make us forget God's presence.

How does this relate to my struggles with rejection? God's presence in our lives fills us with His acceptance and love. The human heart can't go very long without either of these.

But if there's an area of my life where I turn away from the direction of His truth—perhaps a place where I've been hurt by rejection and started believing lies about my God and who I am in Him—I deny myself the protection of His truth. And my search for love and acceptance outside of God's presence then leads to dangerous places. The world's plan always leads us to places of pain, loneliness, and a deep ache for belonging that seems just out of reach.

Because the need to be loved and accepted runs so deep, we find ourselves doing things we never thought possible just to try to satisfy those desires. What starts off as a seemingly small compromise can easily become a complete contradiction to the people we long to be. We set things in motion that we never intended, all because we missed the miracle of His presence and promise in the midst of the mess.

One of the most heartbreaking things I set in motion in my early twenties was justifying the choice to sometimes allow my boyfriend to stay the night in my apartment. Though I wasn't living for the Lord, I knew this was wrong. I'd been to enough church youth groups to have been exposed to the truth about why this wasn't a wise choice.

But instead of applying truth, I justified my desires.

I've met many girls who could tell the same story. For some of us, we justified this because we didn't want to be alone. We didn't want to let go of the good feeling that "he actually wants to be with me." *Finally, I'm not being rejected. I want as much of this acceptance as I can get.* Or, maybe staying over is what he wanted and we didn't want to risk his rejection by saying no. Whatever the case, we brushed aside what we knew was best for what felt best in that moment of vulnerability.

For me, it started small. He slept on the couch and I slept in my bed. But this seemingly small compromise set into motion what needed to remain still since we weren't married. This small compromise opened the door for more compromise. More compromise brought about more justifications. More justifications brought about more compromise, and it all just spiraled out of control.

Then came the day I walked into my bathroom, shaking so badly I could hardly function. I pulled the little stick out of the box. I took the test. I was pregnant. My world started spinning in a haze of desperation. For several weeks I walked around feeling like a shadow. Dark. Hollow. Flat.

I was slowly imploding under the weight of my choices. I had constant panic attacks where I'd claw at my throat while gasping for air. I wanted to run away, but there was no place where reality couldn't find me.

Sin has a horrible appetite. It calls for more and more sin to be set in motion. The only answer I could figure out was an abortion. It all started out small. But what it set in motion grew to be devastatingly huge.

I had the truth. But I had not applied the truth. Therefore, my mind did what my feelings wanted. The decision in that moment was made with a mind conformed to what seemed acceptable to the world. It was not made by a mind transformed by the truth.

According to Romans 12:2, the only way to know God's best for you is not to let your thinking be conformed to the patterns of the world but to be transformed by the renewing of your mind. Then you will be able to discern God's will. That renewing is not a brief spiritual inspiration that comes from brushing up against the truth. It is *anakainosis*, which is a change of heart and life. A heart softened by God's truth. And a life transformed by the application of God's truth.

Let me reach out of this flat page right now and grasp your hand. Feel the tenderness in my touch and the sincerity in what I'm about to say.

Remember Jesus' response to the disciples who missed Him, who cried out in fear, not faith, and, in their terrified state, set into motion all kinds of unnecessary anxiety. The Scripture says *immediately* (I love that it was immediate) He spoke to them and said, "Don't be afraid." The word used here means "don't resist me." And He climbed in the boat with them.

He's saying the same thing to you and me. And He's not running from your mess. He's climbing in it to be right there with you.

What happened yesterday can't be changed, but it can be forgiven. That's your miracle in the mess.

The voices of condemnation, shame, and rejection can come at you, but they don't have to reside in you. That's your miracle in the mess.

---

*The voices of condemnation, shame,
and rejection can come at you, but
they don't have to reside in you.*

And the temptations that were so hard to resist in your flesh will be overpowered by your truth-transformed mind. That's your miracle in the mess.

Based on all we've been examining, here are some good questions to ask ourselves when checking the pliability of our hearts in the middle of a messy situation:

Information: Have I sought out God's truth regarding this situation?

Application: Have I applied God's truth without compromise to this situation?

Transformation: Do I now own this truth as a personal
revelation from God to use in future situations
like this?

Imagine the difference this could make with not setting
into motion what needs to remain still.

After sitting at the top of Mount Arbel, meditating on
all that Jesus chose to do despite the rejections and messi-
ness along the way, I stood up from the rock and closed my
eyes. I wanted to write my story differently than that of the
disciples.

I pictured myself in the lake, straining against the pressure
of life. But I was not a conformed girl; I was a transformed
girl. In the midst of whatever hurts and heartbreaks were
disrupting my peace, I saw Him coming. I no longer cried out
in fear; instead I called out in faith. And I was not terrified. I
was calm. Trusting. Anxious for nothing. Because I knew He
was in control and He was for me. He climbed in my boat, and
the winds died down. My heart was safe, because my heart
was soft.

I turned to Psalm 46:1–10 and meditated on all these truths
as I walked down from the mountain. My body was moving
forward from this sweet place, but my soul was so very still.

> God is our refuge and strength,
> an ever-present help in trouble.
> Therefore we will not fear, though the earth give way
> and the mountains fall into the heart of the sea,
> though its waters roar and foam
> and the mountains quake with their surging.

There is a river whose streams make glad the city of God,
    the holy place where the Most High dwells.
God is within her, she will not fall;
    God will help her at break of day.
Nations are in uproar, kingdoms fall;
    he lifts his voice, the earth melts.

The LORD Almighty is with us;
    the God of Jacob is our fortress.

Come and see what the LORD has done,
    the desolations he has brought on the earth.
He makes wars cease
    to the ends of the earth.
He breaks the bow and shatters the spear;
    he burns the shields with fire.
He says, "Be still, and know that I am God."

Chapter 14

≈

Moving Through the Desperate In-Between

It only takes a teaspoon of rejection to drown an otherwise very alive soul with sorrow. Its poisonous flow has such a sharp potency that cuts through skin and bone. In milliseconds it gets into the very core of our chests, causing oxygen to be blocked, and suddenly a hollowed-out urgency for air sets in. We don't give air much thought breath to breath, day to day, until it's taken from us.

Love is like air in that way. When relationships are good there seems to be so much life, we hardly remember what a gift it is. But the minute love packs its things and walks away, the atmosphere seems depleted of all that air. A desperate, wide-eyed panic envelops us right down to the cells of our souls. And we find ourselves choking on utter emptiness.

And the worst horror of all is you're wide-awake for the

entire experience. Though you can feel the best parts of you dying, your collective whole is forced to keep going. And even when time allows you to find your breath again, it leaves behind deeply gnarled scars. Constant reminders that love is doubly edged with the most beautiful potential and the most dangerous pain. Being intimately aware of both means breathing is no longer the effortless habit it once was. Doubt sets in. Fear entangles.

Every breath takes way more effort than it ever did before.

We're no longer standing in that moment of being rejected, but we're not on the other side of it either. It's the desperate in-between. And it's at this exact place where we must make a crucial choice.

If we place our hope and future in the hands of our un-changing, unflinching God who never leaves us or forsakes us, we'll find healing and freedom. We'll be able to see some-thing on the other side of all the pain. Something good. Something we know will be so worth whatever it takes to get well. So instead of running from the pain, we embrace it as necessary. We must feel the pain to heal the pain. If we never allow ourselves to feel it, we won't acknowledge it's there.

We must feel the pain to heal the pain.

Remember: The pain isn't the enemy. Pain is the indica-tor that brokenness exists. Pain is the reminder that the real enemy is trying to take us out and bring us down by keeping us stuck in broken places. Pain is the gift that motivates us to fight with brave tenacity and fierce determination knowing there's healing on the other side.

And in the in-between? Pain is the invitation for God to move in and replace our faltering strength with His. I'm not writing that to throw out spiritual platitudes that sound good; I write it from the depth of a heart that knows it's the only way. We must invite God into our pain to help us survive the desperate in-between.

The only other choice is to run from the pain by using some method of numbing. I've gone this route as well. As a broken-hearted girl in my early twenties, I slipped in and out of the arms of men with whom I knew there was no future. To stop the loneliness I've surrounded myself with people and sought never to be alone. I've also worked ridiculous hours, not to be more productive but to hide behind accomplishments.

Others I've known have used pills, alcohol, and sex. I've also seen people using obsessive methods of controlling everything and everyone in their environments. The options are many. But the results are the same. Numbing the pain never goes to the source of the real issue to make us healthier. It only silences our screaming need for help.

We think we are freeing ourselves from the pain when, in reality, what numbs us imprisons us. If we avoid the hurt, the hurt creates a void in us. It slowly kills the potential for our hearts to fully feel, fully connect, fully love again. It allows the rejection of a person to steal the best potential from every other relationship we desperately want and need.

It even steals the best in our relationship with God. Because instead of Him being our hope, we misplace our hope in people who can't wholly love a desperately broken version of us. Only God can do that. But might I pluck the most glorious truth and plant it right in the middle of your reality?

You aren't that person I just described. Even if you relate

Pain is the

invitation

for God to move in

and replace our

faltering

strength with His.

to some of those numbing attempts and even if you partici-
pated in them an hour ago, it's not you. How do I know that?
You still felt enough pain to pick up this book. And as long as
you are feeling the pain, you want healing from the source of it.

Pain is the sensation that indicates a transformation is
needed. There is a weakness where new strength needs to
enter in. And you have chosen to pursue long-term strength
rather than temporary relief. So don't berate yourself for being
in pain. It just means you are walking toward victory by not
numbing yourself right now.

You are making progress. You aren't going to be stuck in
this. You are going to be strengthened by it, healed from it,
and better off because of it. In Jesus' name, I believe that!

How do we get this new strength? How do we stop ourselves from chasing what will numb us when the deepest
parts of us scream for some relief? How do we not text him
in the late, lonely hours? How do we make the choice to be
alone and be okay with that? How do we stop the piercing
pain of this minute, this hour? How do we function like normal when nothing feels normal at all?

How do we invite God into this desperate in-between?

We invite His closeness.

For me, this means praying. But sometimes when my heart
feels hurt and empty, my words feel quite flat at best, non-
existent at worst. When I feel hurt, I get quiet. To keep my
prayers from feeling forced and insincere, I pray Psalm 91.

It won't take the rejection away. But it will help us press
through it and give us something healthy with which to fill
the desperate in-between. No matter how vast our pit, prayer
is big enough to fill us with the realization of His presence
like nothing else.

I hope with every part of me you'll dare to whisper these ten simple prayers I've written. Fill that empty space with truths tender enough for this raw place. Let His reassurance reset your atmosphere. Let His miraculous mercies wrap their way around you. Let His words of life breathe fresh air into those deep, choking places. And determine to inhale life, fully, deeply, completely once again.

Use these prayers in whatever way is most helpful for you. They could be all strung together in one sitting. Or, you can use them individually for the next five days, praying one in the morning and another at night.

My favorite way to use Scripture-led prayers is to journal my way through them. Record them as you pray them. Then personalize them by adding your own thoughts, personal requests, and inspired insights the Lord gives you. Your own divine revelations will be some of the brightest moments in this whole journey.

Let's pray . . .

Psalm 91

Whoever dwells in the shelter of the Most High
    will rest in the shadow of the Almighty.
I will say of the LORD, "He is my refuge and my fortress,
    my God, in whom I trust."

Surely he will save you
    from the fowler's snare
    and from the deadly pestilence.
He will cover you with his feathers,

and under his wings you will find refuge;
     his faithfulness will be your shield and rampart.
You will not fear the terror of night,
     nor the arrow that flies by day,
nor the pestilence that stalks in the darkness,
     nor the plague that destroys at midday.
A thousand may fall at your side,
     ten thousand at your right hand,
     but it will not come near you.
You will only observe with your eyes
     and see the punishment of the wicked.

If you say, "The LORD is my refuge,"
     and you make the Most High your dwelling,
no harm will overtake you,
     no disaster will come near your tent.
For he will command his angels concerning you
     to guard you in all your ways;
they will lift you up in their hands,
     so that you will not strike your foot against a stone.
You will tread on the lion and the cobra;
     you will trample the great lion and the serpent.

"Because he loves me," says the LORD, "I will rescue him;
     I will protect him, for he acknowledges my name.
He will call on me, and I will answer him;
     I will be with him in trouble,
     I will deliver him and honor him.
With long life I will satisfy him
     and show him my salvation."

1. *"Whoever dwells in the shelter of the Most High"*
Lord, draw me close.

Your Word promises when I draw close to You, You are there. I want my drawing close to be a permanent dwelling place. At any moment when I feel weak and empty and alone, I pray that I won't let those feelings drag me down into a pit of insecurity. But rather, I want those feelings to be triggers for me to immediately lift those burdensome feelings to You and trade them for the assurance of Your security.

I am not alone, because You are with me. I am not weak, because Your strength is infused in me. I am not empty, because I'm drinking daily from Your fullness. You are my dwelling place. And in You I have shelter from every stormy circumstance and harsh reality. I'm not pretending the hard things don't exist, but I am rejoicing in the fact that Your covering protects me and prevents those hard things from affecting me like they used to.

You, the Most High, the name above every rejection, have the final say over me. You know me and love me intimately and personally and fully. Let my reactions to all things make it evident that I spend a lot of time with You. I want my gentleness to be evident to all. I want Your fullness in me to be the atmosphere around me. I want Your love to shine through me. And I want Your peace to be the path I walk. Your truth to be my wisdom when I talk. You are my everyday dwelling place, my saving grace.

Amen.

2. *"Will rest in the shadow of the Almighty"*
   Lord, I receive Your rest.

   I need rest from the incessant hard emotions. Dry my tears. I don't want to bottle up my emotions in any way, but I do want Your help to control them. I don't want my emotions to hold me—or those I do life with—hostage in any way. Help me process what I feel in healthy, productive ways.

   Your shadow is like shade on a hot, scorching day; it's the place where I can acknowledge what I feel. But You give me enough relief that those feelings don't consume me. You are the only one who can do this. No other person or distraction is mighty enough. Forgive me for chasing lesser things.

   Forgive me for trying to get from people a love that only You can give. Yes, I choose to stop the chase and the unhealthy pursuits and place my trust in You. This is the rest I so desperately need.

   Amen.

3. *"I will say of the LORD, 'He is my refuge and my fortress.'"*
   Lord, I am safe with You.

   With You, Lord, I am not afraid. Your shelter and shadow comfort me in my loneliness. I will proclaim out loud, "You are my refuge and my fortress; therefore, I will not fear."

   As a refuge You are my quick place to duck into when fear starts nipping at the edges of my emotions. I close my eyes and proclaim out loud Your promise to be my safe place. I remind fear that I will not entertain his whispered lies. His lies tell me I'll always be alone, and yet Your truth assures me I'm never alone. Not today. Not tomorrow. Not ever. This isn't dependent on a person. It's a security I have in You.

Yes, You are my refuge.

And You are my fortress. A fortress is a strong, high place. It's the place You lift me so fear can no longer have access to me. Fear can't catch what it can no longer reach. What a comfort this is. You lift me high like this when I lift my soul in worship of Your holy name.

Fear can't catch what it can no longer reach.

Worship is what unlocks this high place—the place where fear can't come. Lies flee in the presence of truth. And fear flees with the first utterance of praising Your name. You are my Lord. I bow low to lift You up, my Lord, my love, the protector of my soul.

Amen.

4. *"My God, in whom I trust"*

Lord, I trust You.

With every hope for my future and with every desire of my heart, I trust You, Lord. I trust You, because You have a perfect plan with flawless timing already mapped out. I don't need to figure it out. I just need to stay close to You. Each day You will show me what steps to take. You will guide me toward Your best.

As long as I pursue You and am obedient to You, I know I am right on track. And even when I misstep, Your grace leads me back the minute I turn to You. Forgive me for doubting You. Forgive me for running ahead of You and sometimes lagging behind You.

I'm putting a stake in the ground today, proclaiming the truth that in You I am fully known and I am fully loved. You know me like no other. You love me like no other. And that combination assures me that You know what I need and when I need it. You already stand in my future and see the very best route for me. The path of provision and protection is perfectly designed by my God, in whom I trust.

Amen.

5. "Surely he will save you from the fowler's snare and from the deadly pestilence."

Lord, You will save me.

I will have moments when the enemy has set out traps in secret to snare me and pull me off of Your best path. Just as the fowler has a strategic plan to lure the bird by hiding food in a disguised trap, my enemy wants to lure me. The food is good for the bird but not when it is part of the plan of the fowler. Satan will often take what is good and twist it into a hidden snare.

Help me see these kinds of traps. Help me recognize good things offered but with my Enemy's plans behind them.

My desire for love is good. But if I pursue love in the wrong way, with the wrong person, in the wrong timing, the enemy will trap me. I confess I have allowed this to happen. I ask for forgiveness. The enemy's plans are to steal, kill, and destroy. Give me strength to resist the traps the Enemy has set in my path today.

Lord, give me a keen awareness of the Enemy's schemes. Give me a pure desire for only Your best. Save me from the hurt and heartbreak of following after good things the wrong way.

Amen.

6. *"He will cover you with his feathers, and under his wings you will find refuge; his faithfulness will be your shield and rampart. You will not fear the terror of night, nor the arrow that flies by day, nor the pestilence that stalks in the darkness, nor the plague that destroys at midday."*

Lord, You cover me, and Your faithfulness protects me.

The fowler not only traps birds but also shoots them down with his silent but deadly arrows. Lord, You protect me not only from my enemy's traps but from his direct attacks and assaults as well. It is Your faithfulness that shields me and surrounds me on all sides. This rejection I'm facing right now feels so deeply wounding that it's hard to feel protected. I'm going to stand on truth rather than my feelings and proclaim that this rejection isn't a piercing by the enemy but rather a protection by You.

Your covering has kept me safe, even if I can't see that full picture right now. Baby birds under their mother's wing rarely know the full story of what happens on the outside. They don't need to know the details, and neither do I. If this now broken relationship was Your best, You wouldn't have kept me from it. And if it is Your best sometime in the future, the enemy won't be able to keep us apart.

But for now, I have peace that there's a purpose for

this brokenness. I don't need to control it. I'm just going to embrace it as good for today. Shield me from the enemy's darts of doubt, discouragement, and division. Surround me with your reassurance, inspiration, and unity. Make me brave. Make me steadfast.

Thank You for the certainty of Your protection.

Amen.

7. "A thousand may fall at your side, ten thousand at your right hand, but it will not come near you. You will only observe with your eyes and see the punishment of the wicked. If you say, 'The LORD is my refuge,' and you make the Most High your dwelling, no harm will overtake you, no disaster will come near your tent."

Lord, I say it again with even more assurance: You are my refuge, and I make You my dwelling. Therefore, no harm will overtake me.

Lord, hard things will happen. This situation is hard. But it will not harm me long-term. It will not destroy me. It can be devastating for a season, but it will not be a destructive force in my life story.

Yes, rejection has destroyed others, but Your Word does say it will not overtake those who live what I've been praying. I do proclaim You as my refuge. I do make You my dwelling. Praying this, proclaiming this, and living this makes this my secure promise from You. I praise You for this good word. I praise You for being a promise maker and a promise keeper. Others may break their promises to me, but You never will.

Amen.

8. *"For he will command his angels concerning you to guard you in all your ways; they will lift you up in their hands, so that you will not strike your foot against a stone."*

Lord, I acknowledge Your angels on assignment from You to protect me. Like secret agents, Your angels are guarding me. Thank You for Your careful concern for every part of me—physical, emotional, and spiritual. In all ways, You are with me.

As much as I feel the pull of temptation to chase lesser things in moments of desperation, I know Your angels fight for me. I will not feel alone or powerless in my desperation. I will feel guarded like the treasured daughter I am. I know You are making all things right and good. I know Your love will reign supreme.

Amen.

9. *"You will tread on the lion and the cobra; you will trample the great lion and the serpent."*

Lord, I know the enemy has already been defeated.

I fight from victory, not for victory. You have already won by defeating death and rendering the enemy a fallen foe. I will tread and trample the enemy by reminding him over and over again that he has no place in my life.

No place in my mind.

No place in my decision-making process.

No place in my heart.

No place in my future.

All of me is reserved and preserved for life. Your life. No part of me was made for the death of the enemy.

I declare that my dead places of discouragement and insecurity be made alive by Your resurrection power.

In Jesus' name!

Amen.

10. "Because he loves me," says the LORD, "I will rescue him; I will protect him, for he acknowledges my name. He will call on me, and I will answer him; I will be with him in trouble, I will deliver him and honor him. With long life I will satisfy him and show him my salvation."

Oh, Lord, I do acknowledge Your name.

You are my Savior, my Lord, my leader, my love, my Maker, my friend, my God, my light, my truth, my salvation. Instantly when I call on Your name, Your power is infused into any situation I face.

I believe You will rescue me, protect me, answer me, be with me, deliver me, and honor me with a satisfying life. It's almost too much for me to take in all these promises. I don't deserve all this, but I will receive them as the gifts they are.

I love You, Lord. I reserve the sacred parts of my heart for You alone. I place You above all, in all, around all, and trust You with all. I will not let this heartbreak steal one more moment of my full attention being on You.

When anxiety tries to come back center stage, I will command it to leave in Your name. When doubt and discouragement threaten to weaken my belief in Your goodness, I will proclaim truth and watch the lies scamper like scared pests. When fear tries to steal my focus, I will worship Your holiness and elevate my perspective with Your promises.

Yes, You are with me always and forever. I may be rejected by man, but I am forever cherished and accepted by the Most High God.
Amen.

And with that I close my prayer journal feeling a lot less desperate and a lot more whole. I breathe the atmosphere of life His words bring.

I picture Him standing at the door of my future, knocking. If I will let Him enter into the darkness of my hurt today, He will open wide the door to a much brighter tomorrow. Even the smallest sliver of His light completely destroys the black bleakness of today's troubles. The more light, the more bright my future becomes. I know this now.

I no longer see prayer as a rote spiritual activity. I crave these intimate times with Him. They are my sweetest conversations, knitting me whole again from the inside out. With great enthusiasm I uninvite the enemy's entanglements so I can fully invite my sweet Jesus in.

And I seal all of this as absolute truth in my life by also inviting in one trusted friend. I share with her what I've kept from so many others. That way I have one human voice who can repeat it back to me on those days of doubt. On those off days when life is hard, she can help me stand on the bold faith of today so I don't forget that bold faith is in me.

I pray this desperate in-between ends today. But even if not, I am more whole now than ever before. I breathe ever so deeply and smile with gratitude. I run my finger over my healing scar and no longer see it as the evidence of hurt but rather as a badge of victory.

Chapter 15

I Want to Run Away

You want to know one of the worst feelings in the world to me? Feeling stuck.

Stuck in a situation where I can't see things getting better. I look at the next five minutes, five hours, five days, and all I see are the same hard things being repeated over and over and over.

I try to give myself a little pep rally of sorts and tap into that Pollyanna girl that's inside me somewhere. The part of me that knows the glass is half-full and chooses to see the bright side. But Pollyanna isn't there.

Life suddenly feels like it will be this way forever. Impossible. Hard. Beyond what I can bear. And this dark funk eclipses me. I want to see the light at the end of the tunnel, so to speak. But what if I just feel hopelessly stuck in the very dark middle? The place where the light isn't shining quite yet? And I start wondering if it ever will.

This happened to me when a boy broke my heart in high school. We were best friends, which is usually code for the girl is secretly in love with the boy who enjoys her company but not enough to date her.

Instead of moving my affections elsewhere, I allowed myself to stay stuck in the "friend zone." He enjoyed having me as the friend that was always there for him, helping work through the constant drama of his ever-changing girlfriends.

But it ripped my heart into pieces every time he was on the upswing with a girl and talked about how amazing every aspect of her perfection was. Hearing him say things about other girls I dreamed of him saying about me made every one of my insecurities feel like an exposed, raw nerve.

He cycled through girlfriends like a starved mosquito on sweaty campers without bug spray.

I just kept smiling on the outside while dying on the inside.

Finally, I'd had enough. I asked if we could talk and then drove to his house. It was dusk. Not quite light. Not quite dark. The in-between-day-and-night time seemed like such an appropriate setting for a girl caught in a relationship where she neither felt quite as accepted as she wanted or rejected as she feared.

I walked into his house as I'd done hundreds of times before. But for the first time ever, I forced honesty into the atmosphere of our relationship. I admitted I was in love with him and could no longer pretend that friendship was enough for me. He looked at me with a gaping mouth that, for a brief second, appeared to be about to speak. But when he failed to actually say something, anything, I turned and walked out to my car.

The least I could do was to preserve the tiniest ounce of dignity by being the first to walk away.

In a Hollywood movie, he suddenly would have seen the light and realized he was in love with me, too, about the time I started to pull away from his house. I'd look in the rear-view window, see him waving his arms while chasing my car, throw my car into park, and the credits would roll as the two friends sealed their love with a kiss in the middle of the road.

But this wasn't the movies. This was high school. Not only did he not come after me, but for a long season he stopped talking to me altogether. And though I'm so thankful now I never became just another throwaway girlfriend to him, it was devastating to a young girl with a crush. Love felt like a thing reserved for other people but always slightly out of reach for me.

As I drove my car away that night, I replayed the awful scene of rejection over and over in my mind. My admission of love had been met with a deafening silence that pierced deep places. Each time I replayed it, the rejection seemed more and more intense. I wanted to run away to a place that had never heard this boy's name or mine. Where I could rewrite the script in my mind of what happened, or at least pretend it never had.

And I thought I'd live with that crushing feeling for the rest of my life. The high school boy eventually became a faded memory. Time gave me that gift. But the pain from that rejection seemed to stay very fresh.

There were several other seasons of crushing feelings that I thought would last forever. And every time I felt stuck with a suffocating sense of wanting to feel better but not knowing how. My brain has such a hard time overriding my heart sometimes. One rejection after another did quite a number on my heart. And each new rejection didn't just add hurt; it multiplied the pain that was already there. That accumulation created a dark feeling of hopeless defeat.

Since I didn't understand there could be good that comes from pressing through the pain, I just wanted to run away from it.

The funny thing is, that high school girl thought finding love and getting married would fix all of this. It didn't. People can't fix from the outside a perspective that needs to be rewired on the inside. Only the Lord can do that.

Rejection has long ties pulling the pain of yesterday into the situations of today. What felt hopeless yesterday will feed a hopelessness into today unless we cut those ties.

Running from the pain won't fix it.

Pretending to be fine when you're really not fine won't fix it.

Avoiding future relationships won't fix it.

Staying busy enough or becoming successful enough or accumulating enough won't fix it.

I closed my eyes and said, "Lord, what will fix this? What will take away this feeling that I'm going to be stuck in seasons of darkness the rest of my life?"

Three words popped into my mind: *Turn to Me.*

This sounded good in theory. But in reality *turning to God* felt a bit like trying to hug air. Sometimes it's hard to wrap my mind around something I can't wrap my arms around.

So I picked up the only piece of God I could physically touch: His Word. "If you carefully observe all these commands I am giving you to follow—to love the LORD your God, to walk in obedience to him and to hold fast to him—then the LORD will drive out all these nations before you, and you will dispossess nations larger and stronger than you" (Deuteronomy 11:22–23).

I love how the Scriptures say "hold fast" to the Lord. The

People can't

fix from the outside

a *perspective*

that needs to

be *rewired* on

the inside.

dark funk makes me want to hold slow. Make God the last thing I try when I'm stumbling and falling. But if I close my eyes, turn to Him, and simply whisper, "God . . . ," at the utterance of His name He "dispossesses" things trying to possess me.

He releases the grip of the dark and helps me see this is a part of the tunnel, but it's not the whole journey. It might be dark in this section, but it won't be dark all the way through. But even in the darkest parts, I have immediate access to Him.

In the midst of struggles, He is there . . . I just have to acknowledge that reality. "God, I love You. I don't love this situation. But I love You. Therefore, I have everything I need to keep putting one foot in front of the other and walking through until I get to the other side of this."

One step at a time. With the full assurance God is okay with me even when I'm not okay with me. And I realize, I can't hold on to the desire to run and at the same time go where God wants to lead me.

Jesus Could Have Run

Jesus knew the crushing heart feeling. He felt it. He carried it. He wrestled with it.

And there was a moment when He could have run.

The night was heavy with grief for Him. Jesus ate with the disciples for the very last time. He'd tried to prepare them for what was about to happen, but they didn't really understand.

Judas had left the supper to commit an unthinkable betrayal against his friend, his teacher, his Lord. His feet were still freshly clean from the Lord of heaven and earth bending low to touch his humanity and rinse off the dirt. But the warmth of the best kind of love was soon traded for a handful of cold coins.

And then it was time for Jesus to walk with the other disciples to the place where they'd met so many times. Their gathering place would soon become their scattering place. John 18:1–2: "After saying these things, Jesus crossed the Kidron Valley with his disciples and entered a grove of olive trees. Judas, the betrayer, knew this place, because Jesus had often gone there with his disciples" (NLT).

Judas was on his way with money clinking in his pocket and steps heavy with malicious intent.

Though Jesus had some of the disciples close by, He knew He was utterly alone. Alone in His understanding of the seriousness of the night. Alone in His pain. Alone in His assignment. Jesus said to Peter, James, and John, "My soul is overwhelmed with sorrow to the point of death . . . Stay here and keep watch" (Mark 14:34).

And his only companions fell asleep.

"Going a little farther, he fell to the ground and prayed that if possible the hour might pass from him. 'Abba, Father,' he said, 'everything is possible for you. Take this cup from me . . .'" (Mark 14:35–36).

And right there is the point at which Jesus could have run. He stared at what it meant to press through the events of the cross, and every bit of His humanity cried out, "Take this cup from Me."

An interesting fact about the Garden of Gethsemane is that it sits at the base of a known escape route from the city over the Mount of Olives toward the Judean desert. This is the route David took when running from his son Absalom.

Jesus would have known this. But instead of running, He turned to His Father and said nine hell-shattering, demon-shaking, Devil-killing words: "Yet not what I will, but what you will" (Mark 14:36).

The first time I stood in the Garden of Gethsemane, tears ran down my face. It is rare for me to let my emotions flow so freely. But it felt holy to let my tears fall and become part of the soil cradling these trees. As if it was the only way that some part of me could be personally invested in this place, I willed myself to cry it all out.

And of all the memories that pricked the tears to come, it was the ones with my dad's face that hurt most of all. I saw myself looking at my dad with pleading eyes to write the opening scenes of my life with the theme of love. He chose rejection instead.

That's where I shifted what I then expected from all of life. Instead of looking at life with the hope of receiving love, I started expecting rejection. Even if life handed me love, I suspiciously waited for it to be snatched away. I knew this had to change.

> I couldn't keep letting the rejection of my dad taint my relationship potential today.
> I couldn't keep trying to outrun the hurt.
> I couldn't keep asking God to take this cup from me.
> I couldn't keep thinking that everything about my life would have been better if only my dad would have loved me.

The dark funk that kept cycling in and out of my life was hopelessness.

Steal a girl's hope and you stomp the life out of her sweetest desires.

Maybe you have that one haunting rejection that lingers in your life as well. Like with me, it could be a parent who walked away. Or, it could be a friend, a sibling, a spouse, a mentor, or one of many others who have walked away while tossing your love aside.

I think you know by now, I very much understand on a deep level. And as long as I kept tying everything back to wishing things with my dad had been different, I would be hurt by him forever. I would be incapable of moving forward. I would be stuck in a reality of my past that I was powerless to change.

But if I really believed that God's healing is more powerful than any hurt the world could ever hand me, I could trust God. I could trust His plans. I could move forward by saying, "Yet not what I will, but what You will."

I had to turn to God and say those same nine words as Jesus did. And I couldn't think of a better time and place than this to do just that. Maybe these pages could be your place to say those same words.

The Middle Eastern sun skipped and danced across the greenish-silver leaves of the olive trees. I breathed in the warm air and started:

> *Yet not what I will, but what You will.*
>
> *I trust that in all these things, Your will is good. I can trust You even when I don't understand. I cannot fully trust You while still holding on to things that made me question You. I have to let those things go.*
>
> *You so clearly promise when I am blinded by the dark realities, You will guide me. You will guide me to the*

spiritual help I need. But You will also guide me to the emotional and physical help I need. Help me see Your provisions and be humble enough to receive them. You will make the rough places smooth. You will do these things and will never forsake me.

You have said, "I will lead the blind by ways they have not known, along unfamiliar paths I will guide them; I will turn the darkness into light before them and make the rough places smooth. These are the things I will do; I will not forsake them" (Isaiah 42:16).

You say Your Word is sharper than a double-edged sword. So I cut these ties from my soul with the precise edge of Your truth.

I was abandoned. That is a fact from my past, but it is not the destiny of my future.

I was rejected. That is a fact from my past, but it is not the destiny of my future.

I was hurt. That is a fact from my past, but it is not the destiny of my future.

I was left out. That is a fact from my past, but it is not the destiny of my future.

I was brokenhearted. That is a fact from my past, but it is not the destiny of my future.

Heartbreaking seasons can certainly grow me but were never meant to define me. I let go of the hurt and embrace the growth the minute I'm able to say, "Yet not what I will, but what You will."

Heartbreaking seasons can certainly grow me but were never meant to define me.

Jesus modeled this.

He was betrayed, mocked, abandoned, beaten, crucified, and buried. Those were all facts of His past, but they were not the destiny of His future. His pain in the garden became power in the tomb! His crucifixion on the cross became the defeat of death. His broken body became the resurrection hope for the world.

He did rise!

And so will we.

I stand and I pump my fist! I sing the closing praise song and feel jubilant as this chapter seems to be at a close. But before we stick a bookmark in it and determine we know all there is to know, I want to linger in the garden for just a minute more. There's something else we must learn. After all, there is often a delay between the rejection of Friday and the resurrection of Sunday.

And I don't know about you, but I certainly need perspective to hold on to between the rejection and the resurrection. In the last chapter we discussed what to pray in the desperate in-between times. Now I want to tell you what you must know during the desperate in-between times. That's why I don't think it was a coincidence the olive tree was there in those moments of deep sorrow for Jesus.

Yes, the resurrection was coming! Jesus knew that. But in the moment of being overwhelmed with sorrow, He, too, wrestled.

And what was the setting of this most profound moment? A garden full of olive trees. The olive tree is such a picture of perspective.[1] I believe the Creator of all, who does everything with purpose, chose to be in the shade and shadow of the olive trees often. And possibly didn't just choose to be among the olive trees in His darkest hour, but might He have actually created them for such a time as this?

Yes, the olive tree was more than just a backdrop for Jesus.

The Crushing Times Are Necessary Times

First, in order to be fruitful, the olive tree has to have both the east wind and the west wind. The east wind is the dry, hot wind from the desert. This is a harsh wind. So harsh that it can blow over green grass and make it completely wither in one day. (The east wind is also the one that blew over Job's house.)

The west wind, on the other hand, comes from the Mediterranean. It brings rain and life.

The olive tree needs both of these winds to produce fruit . . . and so do we. We need both the winds of hardship and the winds of relief to sweep across our lives if we are to be truly fruitful.

The Crushing Times Are Processing Times

Another thing to consider about the olive tree is how naturally bitter the olive is and what it must go through to be useful. If you were to pick an olive from the tree and try to eat it, its bitterness would make you sick.

For the olive to be edible, it has to go through a lengthy process, which includes . . .

washing,
breaking,

soaking,
sometimes salting,
and waiting.

It is a lengthy process to be cured of bitterness and prepared for usefulness. If we are to escape the natural bitterness
of the human heart, we have to go through a long process as
well . . . the process of being cured.

The Crushing Times Are Preservation Times

The final thing I want to consider about the olive is the best
way to preserve it for the long run. It must be crushed in
order to extract the oil. The same is true for us. The biblical
way to be preserved is to be pressed. And being pressed can
certainly feel like being crushed.

But what about 2 Corinthians 4:8, where it says, "we are . . .
pressed . . . but not crushed"? Let's read verses 8 and 9 in the
King James Version: "We are troubled on every side, yet not
distressed; we are perplexed, but not in despair; persecuted,
but not forsaken; cast down, but not destroyed."

This was one of the biggest aha moments for me while
standing in the shadow of the olive tree: crushing isn't the
olive's end. Crushing, rather, is the way of preservation. It's
also the way to get what's most valuable, the oil, out of the
olive. Keeping this perspective is how we can be troubled on
every side yet not distressed . . . pressed to the point of being
crushed but not crushed and destroyed.

⌒

I think I need to revisit these truths often:

> When the sorrowful winds of the east blow, I forget they
> are necessary.
> When I'm being processed, I forget it's for the sake of
> ridding me of bitterness.
> And when I'm being crushed, I forget it's for the sake of
> my preservation.

I forget all these things so easily. I wrestle and cry and honestly want to resist and run from every bit of this. Oh, how I forget.

Maybe God knew we all would. And so, He created the olive tree.

The olive tree is such a beautiful reminder that this isn't how it's going to be forever. On the other side of the harsh wind is fruit. On the other side of the process of being broken and waiting is a useful heart free of bitterness. On the other side of being pressed and crushed is oil . . . the most valuable part of me set free to emerge.

On the other side of every hardship is a resurrection.

We must believe that what God has said He will do will be done. Don't focus on the problems. Instead, have the resurrection mind-set that holds fast to God's promises. Good is coming!

---

*On the other side of every
hardship is a resurrection.*

This was true for Jesus. It's true for the olive tree. And it's certainly true for you and me as well. Though my circumstances may not change today, my outlook surely can. I will not run. I will rise above. I will trust God's will above my desires. I will let truth free my soul from ties to past hurts. I will step into today's destiny. And in the doing of this, I see His flicker of light, and a pulse of divine hope courses through my heart.

Chapter 16

❧

What I Thought Would
Fix Me Didn't

I think most of us have a sense that there are secret cures in life. We want a secret pill to make us thin. Or a ten-minute computer game to enable us to speak a second language. Or an overnight cream that erases all evidence of age from our faces and too many potato chips from our thighs.

A little somethin' somethin' that will suddenly make the flab fab, the tongue bilingual, and the wrinkles smooth. We want easy results. Quick fixes. Self-improvements at the speed of a drive-through window.

My whole life I've wanted this kind of easy cure for rejection. Something that would make my soul stop twitching with insecurities and worries of being abandoned. Where, with complete confidence, I can finally say, "I belong!" And this belonging would be permanent. Irrevocable. Without doubt or conditions. Set in cement.

I've spent many a year chasing what I thought would elevate me past feeling left out and lonely. I remember thinking I'd hit upon the jackpot of an answer in third grade.

Third grade was when I first became aware of the divisions between my peers. Those with alligator logos on their preppy shirts and wing-backed hairdos were starting to group together and away from those of us with hand-me-downs, buck teeth, and frizzy hair. My mom always told me I was beautiful, but my peers made me feel like either my mom wasn't able to tell me the truth or she needed better glasses. Either way, though, I desperately wanted to be "in." I was clearly "out" of the popular crowd.

Mrs. Hartung, my third-grade teacher, had a Dorothy Hamill haircut, big round glasses, and a very round tummy that pronounced she might not make it to the end of the year with us if her baby came. She was gentle and sweet. And she liked my writing. She even submitted a speech I wrote for the school contest. It would be a good long while before we knew who won, but just the fact that she smiled on my words made me feel as if she smiled on me.

I don't remember a single classroom lesson she taught, but I very clearly remember the way she made me feel. She gave me hope that the worries weighing me down in the third-grade pecking order of my peers might not always be my reality.

Yes, she made me feel exceptional.

It helped that her husband worked at our local newspaper, proof that her belief in my writing skills was founded on more than a teacher's requirement to see the best in all her students. When I found out we were going on a field trip to Mr. Hartung's place of work, I remember thinking this very well might be the single greatest day of my entire eight-year life.

Mr. Hartung was a bit of a bearded celebrity to me. I remember seeing his thumbnail photo beside an article he'd written one Saturday morning. Right then and there, with Rice Krispies as my witness, I knew this was the answer I'd been looking for. If I was ever able to write stuff and have it appear in the paper with my thumbnail photo, I'd be cured of rejection.

Yes!

I envisioned the delightful egg-and-toast conversations of thousands of my fellow hometown kinfolk simultaneously sipping coffee and drinking in my words. Then they would exhale, "She's brilliant."

And then maybe a marching band would show up on my front door step and confetti would fall from the sky as we all glided to the town square, where the mayor would give me a key to the city. And the popular kids would be cheering. And my hair would unfrizz. And my pearly whites would suddenly and miraculously be preacher-man straight!

I'm incredibly realistic.

I thankfully wasn't privy quite yet to the fact that most people think writers are average at best. And usually it's the critics, not the enamored, who give the most feedback. But I didn't know this at the time, so my fantasy fix-it plan for rejection was well under way. I was surely going to wow those newspaper folks to the point where they'd be convinced their next star columnist was a third grader from Mrs. Hartung's class.

Before I knew it the field trip day arrived. We got off the sticky, hot school bus and lined up in front of the tall building.

I remember the regal white columns. The scripty font on the sign. And the way Mrs. Hartung hushed us before opening the front doors. It might as well have been the gates of heaven. I breathed deeply and prepared to step into a whole new future as the most popular kid in school. Hello, *Tallahassee Democrat*.

Then suddenly a demon in the form of a wasp handpicked me out of all the crowd to attack. I reeled back as pain shot in all directions on my arm. I screamed. Tears trickled down my red cheeks. And my arm swelled up Popeye-style. I never even made it past the lobby. My mom came to get me. And the next day at school I was the brunt of more jokes than ever.

Even months later, when I won the speech contest at school, I can remember being terrified of standing up at the outside assembly to deliver my winning speech. I had no notions of quick fixes or parades or keys to the city suddenly making me popular. I was simply terrified that another wasp would attack me, putting all my fears and tears on display again.

By then I'd learned a painful lesson I'd continue to learn over and over again through the different seasons of my life: The spotlight never fixes our insecurities. It only magnifies what we thought popularity would cover up.

> *The spotlight never fixes our insecurities.*
> *It only magnifies what we thought*
> *popularity would cover up.*

Neither does a great relationship. I have an amazing marriage. (Most of the time.) But there have been seasons when I just about destroyed our relationship, because I was so terrified of him one day leaving me. I imagined affairs that never happened and a whole host of other crazy scenarios that simply weren't true.

It was just like winning that contest but not enjoying it, because I was convinced another wasp was coming at any minute.

The list of things I've thought would fix me through the years goes well beyond popularity and relationships. I imagine you could keep adding things you've attempted here as well. Life just doesn't tie up neatly. There are more wasps and more stings; these things are just part of life. But Jesus doesn't refuse to reach out to us in the middle of hurts and heart-breaks and mess-ups.

Our Lord's divinity has never been hesitant to step into the mess of humanity. He is the great answer to our every desire. And He will not let our need for divine, deep love meant to be fulfilled by Him alone be cheaply met by lesser things. He may very well give us good gifts. He may entrust to us relationships and success and blessings of all kinds. After all, He loves to give good gifts to those He loves. But He will not honor the chase of these things.

If we think lesser things can truly satisfy, we'll forever chase the wind. It's an exhausting search. We're forever out of breath in hot pursuit of becoming someone we perceive we need to be:

"One day I'll become someone's wife."

"One day I'll become someone significant."

"One day I'll live there or drive that or be able to buy things without looking at the price tags."

"One day I'll hit this benchmark of success or brilliance or status."

We say it with such confidence and then chase everything and everyone that can help make this happen. And in the process we run farther and farther away from the only Giver of good gifts. The One who wants to live a love story with us. Not as the magic genie we occasionally run to for a little dose of divine help. But the One who stills us, quiets us, wipes away our exhaustion, and whispers:

"It's not about you *becoming* anything. Your soul was made to simply *be* with Me. And the more you are with Me, the more you will stop fearing what the world might take from you. With Me you are free to be you. The real you. The you honesty called to at the very beginning of this journey. The you whose core is in alignment with My truth. The you who doesn't fear imperfections or rejections, because grace has covered those in the loveliest of ways."

Overcoming rejection can never be dependent on overcoming a perceived obstacle. "I want that, and if I get it, life will be great." No. Oh, God, cripple the part of our hearts that dares misguide us with this thinking.

The deepest part of me runs to find honesty. And when I find honesty, I realize it was Jesus calling to me all along. I get it now. I finally get it. I'm vulnerable, but I'm deeply assured.

And with an embrace that rivals any ever given, I exclaim, "Rejection never has the final say. Rejection may be a delay or distraction or even a devastation for a season. But it's never a final destination. I'm destined for a love that can't ever be diminished, tarnished, shaken, or taken. With You, Jesus, I'm forever safe. I'm forever accepted. I'm forever held. Completely loved and always invited in."

With You, Jesus,

I'm forever safe.

I'm forever accepted.

I'm forever held.

Completely loved

and always invited in.

What's It Like to Do Life with Me?

Hi friend,

I am so honored to have walked through this book with you. As I wrote this message, I cried through some parts and rolled my eyes laughing at other parts . . . but most of all I thought of you with every word.

Though we may never have met in person, God gave me a profound sense of compassion for you as He poured this message through my heart and into every typed word. I deeply understand the hurt that haunts the heart of the one rejected.

I pray you could feel my love for you on every page. I wrote this message because I needed it most of all. But I pray my thoughts and revelations from Jesus have comforted you and helped you in wonderfully freeing ways.

Now that we've been honest and courageous with looking at rejection from all angles, there's one last part I want us to consider. In the midst of rejection, it's so hard to think that we might be doing something to add to the situation. It's usually much easier to identify where others have gone wrong and hurt us. But now that we've made progress together in *Uninvited*, this is a safe place to really analyze ourselves by asking the question, "What's it like to do life with me?"

So I wrote a bonus chapter to help us process through this. Honestly, I might have written this chapter just for me. Because y'all. For real. I've got blind spots. And the people who live in close proximity to me are probably more aware of them than I am.

But just in case you think it could be for you, too, this chapter is here along with a small assessment you can take afterward.

So if you're feeling brave, let's intentionally open our hearts. Ask the Lord to show us what He wants to speak to us. And then turn the page together.

Much love,
Lysa

It's a fascinating question: What's it really like to do life with me? I want the answer to be: *Amazing! Wonderful! The best!*

And in some moments, maybe that's true. But each time I'm uninvited, it's a good time to take a step back and re-evaluate some things. And not just about the other person. I think most of us have the propensity to believe it was the other person's issues that caused her to reject us. And maybe that's true. But I think a more productive use of time is to reevaluate some things about us.

I've tripped through enough relationship potholes to know I bring my own set of imperfections and complications. I could just explain away the hard realities of barriers and break-downs with others, or I could attempt to look at some possible patterns within myself and pay attention. And by paying attention I mean listen, really listen.

There is a story my past needs to tell my present.

And honestly, there are probably a few things others have tried to tell me that I couldn't or wouldn't hear. I gave this some serious thought when I was inspired by a new friend who had physical hearing challenges.

I was at a church conference, sitting backstage feeling the usual pre-message jitters, when the event coordinator asked if I would wear an oblong plastic device hooked to my shirt. Thinking this was a modern version of a lapel microphone, I explained that I was just using a handheld mic so there was no need for a clip-on.

An anxious look crossed her face. She went on to explain that there was a woman in the audience who asked if I would wear this as a special favor so she could better hear my message.

I wanted to do this for the audience member, no question.

But not really understanding the situation, I grew concerned. I didn't want my blouse to droop or pull in places that would make me hyperconscious, and there didn't seem to be any inconspicuous way to wear the new device. Trust me, I've been in many an embarrassing situation while standing onstage, and I try to avoid adding any more stories like these to my life.

Thinking of other possible solutions, I went to find the sound guy. I asked him if I could clip the device onto the podium or my Bible as long as I stayed close enough for it to still properly work.

That's when I got more explanation.

For forty-five years, the lady in the audience had never been able to hear a sermon being preached. She'd actually never even heard a prayer being prayed. Her doctor had been working on this special device that would send the specially magnified sound of my voice directly into her hearing aids, allowing her to listen as never before.

Me wearing this clip wasn't just a special favor. This was an epic event in the life of this woman. Now that I'd heard the whole story, I felt like such a heel for worrying about my shirt. I clipped the device directly below my chin and suddenly couldn't have cared less about the shirt droop.

I walked onstage and immediately asked my new friend if she could hear me. With blinking eyes and a huge smile, she nodded. Several times during my message, she had tears streaming down her face. So did her friend with her. By the time I concluded with a prayer, I knew this was an incredible victory for her lifelong struggle.

It's amazing what a gift it is to be able to hear. I guarantee you, of all the hundreds of people in the audience that day, there was no one listening with more intentionality than my friend with the device. She knew she needed help to hear. The device helped fill a gap she couldn't fill on her own. Once she made use of it, she was able to listen . . . really listen.

I wish there was a device I could wear to help me become a better listener. Not a better listener because I have trouble hearing. No, I'm talking about really listening to make me more self-aware of the things I referred to earlier that I'm sure others wish I would hear.

To listen or to fail to listen is my choice. Just like when the prophet Ezekiel was being called by God. He was warned that the exiles were unyielding, hardened, and rebellious. "Go now to your people in exile and speak to them. Say to them, 'This is what the Sovereign LORD says,' whether they listen or fail to listen" (Ezekiel 3:11). These people weren't willing to listen to the prophet, because ultimately they weren't willing to listen to God. Ouch.

I never want this to be said about me. But I must admit there are times I don't hear what others are trying to say.

This isn't a fun chapter to write. After all, in the context of this book about healing from rejection, I don't want to have to look internally. It feels a little better to blame others for making me feel left out and lonely. It's hard to say, "I may be part of the issue here." But if I want things to get better for me, I need to take a hard look at me.

The most frustrated people are those who feel their lives can only improve when others put forth the necessary effort to make things better. That's problematic since we can't control others. A more productive view of change is to look at ways we need to change. Yes, others may need to make tweaks too. For now, however, let's take some steps forward to examine ourselves and listen to what this may reveal.

Back to my original question, "What is it really like to do life with me?"

There is a wonderful set of verses in Proverbs 4:20–27. I like looking at the book of Proverbs as a way to examine my current thinking against the backdrop of God's true wisdom. I guess you could say it serves as a spiritual listening device to aid in me being able to hear truth. "Proverbs provides both a goal and route. The goal is successful living and the route is the way of wisdom."[1]

If my goal is to pursue more successful relationships, this wisdom from Proverbs is a great route to take. Proverbs 4:20–22 is a call to wisdom:

> My son, pay attention to what I say;
>   turn your ear to my words.
> Do not let them out of your sight,
>   keep them within your heart;
> for they are life to those who find them
>   and health to one's whole body.

Verses 23–27 are like a checklist of sorts:

❏ Above all else, guard your heart, for everything you do flows from it.

❏ Keep your mouth free of perversity; keep corrupt talk far from your lips.

❏ Let your eyes look straight ahead; fix your gaze directly before you.

❏ Give careful thought to the paths for your feet and be steadfast in all your ways. Do not turn to the right or the left; keep your foot from evil.

Let's unpack this checklist.

"Above All Else, Guard Your Heart, for Everything You Do Flows from It"

This Deals with My Attitude

Have you ever interacted with a know-it-all? Know-it-alls see themselves as a resident expert on almost every topic and are very bold with their opinions. As a matter of fact, they don't see the thoughts they express as opinions at all. They feel all that they share are absolute facts and aren't shy about shooting down contradictory ideas.

Does someone's face pop into your mind as you read that description? Me too! Actually, a couple of people fall into that description for me. Now, mentally shift your criticism of them to a place of grace for a bit. And let your own picture be the one you see matched with this description.

I know, I know, this doesn't perfectly describe you. But what piece of it does? Usually at least one relationship we have brings out little bits of the know-it-all in us. Seek to see it, even if it's just a hint of it, and determine to try something the next time it starts happening:

Guard your heart from the many slippery slopes.

One of the most damaging elements in relationships is pride. That need to be the expert, the right one, the most knowledgeable—it pulls us down into a pit of pride we probably would never label as such. And because pride is so hard to see, here's a hint of how to know it's there: The less we feel we need to address pride in our lives, the more it has already blinded us.

The less we feel we need to address
pride in our lives, the more it
has already blinded us.

Gracious, that's a painful sentence for me to type. Because it forces me to examine something I quite simply don't want to see or acknowledge. But here are some verses that help me pray through this as I ask God to pry open my spiritual eyes and ears:

- "His pride led to his downfall. He was unfaithful to the LORD his God" (2 Chronicles 26:16).
- "In his pride the wicked man does not seek him; in all his thoughts there is no room for God" (Psalm 10:4).
- "For the sins of their mouths, for the words of their lips, let them be caught in their pride" (Psalm 59:12).
- "When pride comes, then comes disgrace, but with humility comes wisdom" (Proverbs 11:2).
- "Where there is strife, there is pride, but wisdom is found in those who take advice" (Proverbs 13:10).
- "Pride goes before destruction, a haughty spirit before a fall" (Proverbs 16:18).

We must guard our hearts against pride. Otherwise pride will taint everything else we do, say, and think. There are certainly other things we need to guard our hearts from, but pride is so blinding we'll never see them or be receptive to hearing them if we don't address this first. Then we can see and hear the other things with humility.

"Keep Your Mouth Free of Perversity; Keep Corrupt Talk Far from Your Lips"

This Deals with My Propensity Toward or Away from Affirmation

Do our words build up or tear down?

Imagine there is a bridge over a vast canyon. You are on one side, and a person you care about is on the other side. Every time you dishonor that person with your words, you remove a plank from the bridge. At first this can seem like no big deal. You can navigate around the gaps by stepping over them. But eventually the gaps become gaping holes, causing the journey to the other person to be a treacherous one. Crossing over starts to feel more and more impossible.

That's a daunting picture, right?

If I want to keep my connecting bridge strong, there are things I need to assess about the way I'm using my words. Things like:

- Questioning actions without having all the facts
- Assuming the worst about intentions instead of believing the best
- Having a critical tone when discussing possibilities for someone's future
- Needing to say "I told you so" when someone takes a wrong turn

- Competing with another person's accomplishments instead of celebrating them
- Processing my thoughts about someone with others before talking directly to that person
- Seeing someone's issues with bold spotlight clarity while thinking mine are but mere shadows in comparison

Each of these things removes the planks one by one from our connecting bridge. The holes can be repaired, but it will take time and great intentionality to build back with affirmation what negativity has eroded. Here are some affirming questions to start with:

- "Would you help me understand how best to encourage you?"
- "When we don't agree, what's the best way to approach a compromise?"
- "What is something you wish I wouldn't do when we discuss issues?"
- "Is there an area of your life I can better support?"
- "What is something in your life you wish we could celebrate together?"
- "How can we make our relationship more of a priority in this season?"
- "Is there a mutual confidant, friend, or counselor who is mature enough to help us think through and strategize ways to improve our relationship?"

This is just the beginning of a positive list. Keep adding to it as you continue to think through this. These affirming planks will go a long way in putting your words to good use!

"Let Your Eyes Look Straight Ahead; Fix Your Gaze Directly Before You"

This Challenges My Altitude

A friend of mine recently told me she put herself through a 360 evaluation. I thought that sounded interesting, so I asked her to explain. Basically, to increase her ability to see things from another person's vantage point, she had to circle the issue, looking for her own blind spots.

As a follower of Jesus, we are followers of wisdom. Fixing our gaze directly before us and looking straight ahead helps us to focus on wisdom and not get deceived by our own blindness and assumptions. I get distracted from wisdom and attracted to foolishness when I don't seek to understand what other people really want.

Wisdom seeks to see someone else's vantage point even if I don't agree with that person's perspective. But only from their perspectives can you strategize about how to meet the other people on common ground. Foolishness refuses to acknowledge there's any other way to look at something but mine. Eventually, others will build barriers to shut this kind of exhausting foolishness out of their lives.

My husband and I have really had to work on this with our relationship. I'm a get-it-done-and-figure-out-the-small-details-later kind of girl. He's a write-out-every-step-because-no-detail-is-too-small-to-become-a-big-problem kind of guy.

Recently, we were helping one of our adult kids think through the purchase of her first little starter home. My daughter and I crunched all the numbers to get to what would be a reasonable monthly mortgage payment. And then we estimated all the other related monthly bills and were good to go. We found a

Wisdom seeks

to see someone else's

vantage point even

if I don't agree with

that person's *perspective*.

great deal on a house that fit within her established budget and felt that we'd attended to all the necessary details.

I thought Art would be thrilled with all our processing when we verbally presented everything to him looking for his support. He wanted everything written out on paper from start to finish. I could have pushed back, confident we'd done what we needed to do, and then just left him out of the rest of the process.

But as I forced myself to look at things from his vantage point, I saw the wisdom in taking the time to write everything out in much more detail than our simple version of running the numbers. We didn't get as detailed as he would have, but we met on the common ground of getting much more on paper than before.

Rising above my own vantage point to circle around and see his was a better altitude from which to see the bigger picture. Had I dug my heels in and refused to meet Art in the common ground, we would have missed some expenses that eventually could have caused our daughter some financial setbacks. In the end we adjusted her remodel budget and were able to set her up for success.

> "Give Careful Thought to the Paths for Your Feet and Be Steadfast in All Your Ways. Do Not Turn to the Right or the Left; Keep Your Foot from Evil."

This Is About My Actions

Okay, last evaluation. Now that we've been diligent with our attitude, affirmation, and altitude, we must analyze our *actions* past and present. Sometimes when I've veered from wisdom, I have to go back to reevaluate past actions in order to go forward in restoring present relationships. To do this we must backtrack, back up, and back down.

- **Backtrack**: Admit we've been wrong. If we're brave enough to start the restoration process by owning one issue where we were wrong, it will start to soften other hard places.
- **Back up**: Ask for forgiveness. This will give the other person a safe place to stand while considering the next step.
- **Back down**: Intentionally show that person the action for which we asked for forgiveness is an area where we are making strides of improvement and breaking unhealthy patterns.

I'm very thankful God's Word helps me see things I need to pay attention to.

Nothing will give you emotional laryngitis like living in close proximity to someone who refuses to listen. Having emotions but no voice chokes the life out of relationships. How tragic for the one silenced. But also, how tragic for the silencer, who throws so much richness of relationship away.

Whew . . . we've covered a lot in this bonus section. I don't picture these pages to be a one-read section. I know I'll revisit all we've just processed again and again as I make progress in various relationships. Learning to listen requires strategies to improve our hearing. Just as my friend's life changed when she was given a hearing device, I pray this section gives you a relationship revitalization.

And the next time you ask the question, "What's it really like to do life with me?" I pray the answer makes you and those you love smile.

What's It Like to Do Life
with Me? Assessment

INSTRUCTIONS: You read "What's It Like to Do Life with Me?" and now it's time to really assess this in your personal life. Next to each statement in the list, note whether that statement is true or false for you the majority of the time. Then, cover your responses and have a trusted friend or family member write their answers about you on the other page. At the end, prayerfully compare the two sets of answers to see what it's really like to do life with you. Make sure you both have time after doing the assessment to talk about your responses and how you might be able to improve in the areas that need attention.

Pray this before comparing both sets of answers:

Lord, thank You for the gift of refinement. Thank You for extending grace to me because I so desperately need it. Thank You for _____, who so lovingly wants to help me become a better version of me. I pray You'll give me the heart to read these answers without hesitation, hurt, or bias. Help me to see Your guidance through this assessment, and show me areas where I can grow. I want to bring the fullness of Your presence everywhere I go, to everyone I meet. In Jesus' name, amen.

ASSESS YOURSELF

TRUE	FALSE	
		My friends and family know they can count on me to encourage and support them.
		I am easily approachable and others are able to confront me when I've offended them.
		I am the first to apologize.
		I am quick to extend grace and understanding.
		In a conversation, I listen well and wait for my turn to speak.
		I am more oriented toward giving grace and have difficulty speaking truth.
		I am more oriented toward speaking truth and have difficulty giving grace.
		I acknowledge others when they have a better idea than mine.
		Others feel that I understand and respect their opinions even if I disagree.
		I celebrate the success of others, even when I may not experience success of my own.
		I process my thoughts before speaking directly to someone, especially in a heated discussion.
		I assume the best instead of the worst.
		I remain my authentic self regardless of my surroundings.
		I am quick to forgive without holding grudges.
		There are topics or negative emotions that I avoid discussing.

OTHERS' ASSESSMENT OF YOU

TRUE	FALSE	
		I know I can count on my friend to encourage and support me.
		My friend is easily approachable and it's easy for me to confront him/her when he/she has done something wrong.
		My friend is the first to apologize.
		My friend is quick to extend grace and understanding.
		In a conversation, my friend listens well and waits for his/her turn to speak.
		My friend is more oriented toward giving grace and has difficulty speaking truth.
		My friend is more oriented toward speaking truth and has difficulty giving grace.
		My friend acknowledges others when they have a better idea than him/her.
		I feel that my friend understands and respects my opinion even if he/she disagrees.
		My friend celebrates the success of others, even when he/she may not experience success of his/her own.
		My friend processes his/her thoughts before speaking directly to someone, especially in a heated discussion.
		My friend assumes the best instead of the worst.
		I can trust my friend to be authentic, regardless of his/her surroundings.
		My friend is quick to forgive without holding grudges.
		There are topics or negative emotions that my friend avoids.

For more helpful resources and a printable version of this assessment, please visit www.uninvitedbook.com.

CORRECTIVE EXPERIENCE CHART

There is redemption on the other side of rejection using the promises of God. This has been one of the sweetest comforts to my soul when I learned to shift my focus from hurt to hope with God's tender truths. Here's how. In the left column below, write down feelings you have related to rejection. Then in the right column below, write out a promise from Scripture that can redirect that feeling. Some sample promises are listed below, or you can find others with your own search of the Scriptures.

FEELING	PROMISE FROM SCRIPTURE
Example:	
Unwanted	*For you are a people holy to the LORD your God. Out of all the peoples on the face of the earth, the LORD has chosen you to be his treasured possession. (Deuteronomy 14:2 NIV)*
	Other possibilities:
	Psalm 34:5–9, 18; Psalm 37:4; Psalm 91:1; Isaiah 43:1–3; Isaiah 61; Zephaniah 3:17; John 15:7; Romans 8:31–39; Philippians 1:6; Hebrews 13:5–6

FEELING	PROMISE FROM SCRIPTURE

Choose one of the promises you identified above. Write it somewhere you will see it multiple times a day. I have also found it helpful to read these promises aloud until they become the new script for my heart and mind. For a printable version of this chart, please visit www.uninvitedbook.com.

A Note from Lysa

Sweet friend,

For some of you this book will be exactly what you needed to walk you through a hard season or help you heal some past wounds. But for some this book might be the starting place for your healing. Because I'm not a licensed counselor and this book doesn't take the place of therapy, please know there are some difficult realities in life that you *will* want a licensed Christian counselor to help you navigate. Please be honest about your need for counseling help. I am so thankful for the professionals who have lovingly helped lead me through my darkest days. It's always been important to me that the professional counselors I've seen have a deeply committed personal relationship with Jesus and who understand the battle must be fought in both the physical and spiritual realm. I'm praying for you dear friend and I trust you'll be praying for me as well.

Much love,

Lysa

Acknowledgments

My greatest desire in writing *Uninvited* was to tenderly tackle the hard subject of rejection using biblical truths and perspectives because I personally needed those revelations. Over the years, I had slowly started to see that rejections from my past were affecting me more than I realized. And I was handling present day rejections (big and small) with compounded hurt.

I'm thankful that the Lord placed people in my life to process those feelings with and share their own hurts as well. In various ways, their fingerprints dance all inside this book. I thank God for weaving these lives into mine.

Art . . . thank you for being the safe place for my heart to land. I love you.

Jackson, Amanda, Mark, Theresa, Hope, Michael, Ashley, David, Brooke, Paige, and Philecia . . . my priority blessings and added blessings whom I love so very much.

Colette . . . the impact of your friendship on my life is immeasurable. Thank you for always inviting me in and providing the beautiful home where so many of these words were penned.

Leah, Lindsay, Kristen, Kimberly . . . I couldn't do this without your love, laughter, and talents.

Meredith . . . you are truly amazing and gifted beyond measure.

Barb, Lisa A., Glynnis, Amy, Danya, Melissa, Alison, Lindsey, Kaley, Meg, Krista, Lauren, Whitney, and all the Proverbs 31 Ministries gals . . . the best team.

The P31 Board . . . the smartest people I know.

Pastor and my family at Elevation . . . doing life with you is a gift.

Pastor Chris and Tammy . . . I treasure you both so very much. Thank you for welcoming me into your family with such unconditional love and acceptance.

Lisa C. and Lori G. . . . . sweet blessings from God.

The "In the Loop" Group . . . you make ministry so very fun and meaningful.

Jeff, Tiffany, Aryn, Stephanie, Brian, Jessica, Janene, Chad . . . it's one of my greatest joys to work with you all.

Scriptures

Chapter 2: Three Questions We Must Consider

[I am one of] God's chosen people, holy and dearly
loved. (Colossians 3:12)

God saw all that he had made, and it was very good. And
there was evening, and there was morning—the sixth
day. (Genesis 1:31)

"[The world is in] bondage to decay" or "[in] slavery to
corruption." (Romans 8:21 NIV, NASB, THE VOICE)

For the Eternal is on His way:
    yes, He is coming to judge the earth.
He will set the world right by His standards,
    and by His faithfulness, *He will examine* the people.
(PSALM 96:13 THE VOICE)

And we know that in all things God works for the good of those who love him, who have been called according to his purpose. (Romans 8:28)

Those who live according to the flesh have their minds set on what the flesh desires; but those who live in accordance with the Spirit have their minds set on what the Spirit desires. The mind governed by the flesh is death, but the mind governed by the Spirit is life and peace. (Romans 8:5–6)

You will keep in perfect peace
    those whose minds are steadfast,
    because they trust in you.
Trust in the LORD forever,
    for the LORD, the LORD himself, is the Rock eternal.
(ISAIAH 26:3–4)

Chapter 3: There's a Lady at the Gym Who Hates Me

The LORD your God is in your midst,
    a mighty one who will save;
he will rejoice over you with gladness;
    he will quiet you by his love;
he will exult over you with loud singing.
(ZEPHANIAH 3:17 ESV)

"If you abide in Me, and My words abide in you, ask whatever you wish, and it will be done for you." (John 15:7 NASB)

Delight yourself in the LORD,

> and he will give you the desires of your heart.

(PSALM 37:4 ESV)

He who dwells in the secret place of the Most High shall remain stable and fixed under the shadow of the Almighty [Whose power no foe can withstand]. (Psalm 91:1 AMPC)

He appointed twelve that they might be with him and that he might send them out to preach and to have authority to drive out demons. (Mark 3:14–15)

Chapter 4: Alone in a Crowded Room

For this reason I kneel before the Father, from whom every family in heaven and on earth derives its name. I pray that out of his glorious riches he may strengthen you with power through his Spirit in your inner being, so that Christ may dwell in your hearts through faith. And I pray that you, being rooted and established in love, may have power, together with all the Lord's holy people, to grasp how wide and long and high and deep is the love of Christ, and to know this love that surpasses knowledge— that you may be filled to the measure of all the fullness of God. (Ephesians 3:14–19)

But what happens when we live God's way? He brings gifts into our lives, much the same way that fruit appears in an orchard—things like affection for others, exuberance about life, serenity. We develop a willingness to stick with things, a sense of compassion in the heart, and a conviction that a basic holiness permeates things and people. We find ourselves involved in loyal commitments, not needing to force our way in life, able to marshal and direct our energies wisely.

Legalism is helpless in bringing this about; it only gets in the way. Among those who belong to Christ, everything connected with getting our own way and mindlessly responding to what everyone else calls necessities is killed off for good—crucified.

Since this is the kind of life we have chosen, the life of the Spirit, let us make sure that we do not just hold it as an idea in our heads or a sentiment in our hearts, but work out its implications in every detail of our lives. (Galatians 5:22–25 THE MESSAGE)

Chapter 5: Hello, My Name Is Trust Issues

The LORD is my shepherd, I lack nothing.
He makes me lie down in green pastures,
he leads me beside quiet waters,
    he refreshes my soul.
He guides me along the right paths
    for his name's sake.
Even though I walk
    through the darkest valley,
I will fear no evil,
    for you are with me;

your rod and your staff,
    they comfort me.

You prepare a table before me
    in the presence of my enemies.
You anoint my head with oil;
    my cup overflows.
Surely your goodness and love will follow me
    all the days of my life,
and I will dwell in the house of the Lord
    forever.

(Psalm 23)

What, then, shall we say in response to these things? If God is for us, who can be against us? (Romans 8:31)

For God has said, "I will never fail you. I will never abandon you." So we can say with confidence, "The Lord is my helper, so I will have no fear. What can mere people do to me?" (Hebrews 13:5–6 NLT)

The Lord is my light and my salvation—whom shall I fear? The Lord is the stronghold of my life—of whom shall I be afraid? (Psalm 27:1)

Chapter 6: Friendship Breakups

For our struggle is not against flesh and blood, but against the rulers, against the authorities, against the powers of this dark world and against the spiritual forces of evil in the heavenly realms. (Ephesians 6:12)

Chapter 7: When Our Normal Gets Snatched

"On me alone, my lord, be the blame." (1 Samuel 25:24 NASB)

Chapter 8: The Corrective Experience

"Who is this David? Who is this son of Jesse? Many servants are breaking away from their masters these days. Why should I take my bread and water, and the meat I have slaughtered for my shearers, and give it to men coming from who knows where?"

David's men turned around and went back. When they arrived, they reported every word. (1 Samuel 25:10–12)

"Please forgive your servant's presumption. The LORD your God will certainly make a lasting dynasty for my lord, because you fight the LORD's battles, and no wrongdoing will be found in you as long as you live. Even though someone is pursuing you to take your life, the life of my lord will be bound securely in the bundle of the living by the LORD your God, but the lives of your enemies he will hurl away as from the pocket of a sling." (1 Samuel 25:28–29)

Chapter 9: Why Does Rejection Hurt So Much?

When pride comes, then comes disgrace, but with
humility comes wisdom. (Proverbs 11:2)

Humble yourselves, therefore, under God's mighty hand,
that he may lift you up in due time. (1 Peter 5:6)

And he gives grace generously. As the Scriptures say,
"God opposes the proud but gives grace to the humble."
(James 4:6 NLT)

Before a downfall the heart is haughty, but humility
comes before honor. (Proverbs 18:12)

"If my people, who are called by my name, will humble
themselves and pray and seek my face and turn from
their wicked ways, then I will hear from heaven,
and I will forgive their sin and will heal their land."
(2 Chronicles 7:14)

"I [John the Baptist] am not the Anointed One; I am the
one who comes before Him. . . . He, *the groom*, must take
center stage; and I, *the best man*, must step to His side."
(John 3:28–31 THE VOICE)

"That's why my cup is running over. This is the assigned
moment for him to move into the center, while I slip off
to the sidelines." (John 3:29–30 THE MESSAGE)

There is a time for everything, and a season for every activity under the heavens . . . a time to be silent and a time to speak. (Ecclesiastes 3:1, 7)

"Lord Almighty, if you will only look on your servant's misery and remember me, and not forget your servant . . . then I will . . ." (1 Samuel 1:11)

Because the Lord had closed Hannah's womb, her rival [Peninnah] kept provoking her in order to irritate her. (1 Samuel 1:6)

So *in the course of time* Hannah became pregnant and gave birth to a son. (1 Samuel 1:20, emphasis added)

Chapter 10: Her Success Does Not Threaten Mine

For as he thinks in his heart, so is he. (Proverbs 23:7 NLV)

But thanks be to God, who always leads us in triumph in Christ, and manifests through us the sweet aroma of the knowledge of Him in every place. (2 Corinthians 2:14 NASB)

Be fruitful and multiply. (Genesis 1:28 THE VOICE)

If you have bitter jealousy and selfish ambition in your hearts, do not boast and be false to the truth. This is not the wisdom that comes down from above, but is earthly, unspiritual, demonic. (James 3:14–15 ESV)

And God is able to bless you abundantly, so that in all things at all times, having all that you need, you will abound in every good work. (2 Corinthians 9:8)

Let each of you look not only to his own interests, but also to the interests of others. (Philippians 2:4 ESV)

"The harvest is great, but the workers are few. So pray to the Lord who is in charge of the harvest; ask him to send more workers into his fields." (Luke 10:2 NLT)

Chapter 11: Ten Things You Must Remember When Rejected

I will extol the LORD at all times;
    his praise will always be on my lips.
I will glory in the LORD;
    let the afflicted hear and rejoice.
Glorify the LORD with me;
    let us exalt his name together.

I sought the LORD, and he answered me;
    he delivered me from all my fears.

(PSALM 34:1–4)

Those who look to him are radiant;
    their faces are never covered with shame.

(PSALM 34:5)

I say to myself, "The LORD is my portion; therefore I will wait for him." The LORD is good to those whose hope is in him, to the one who seeks him; it is good to wait quietly for the salvation of the LORD. (Lamentations 3:24–26)

The angel of the LORD encamps around those who fear him,
    and he delivers them.
Taste and see that the LORD is good;
    blessed is the one who takes refuge in him.
Fear the LORD, you his holy people,
    for those who fear him lack nothing.
The lions may grow weak and hungry,
    but those who seek the LORD lack no good thing.
                         (PSALM 34:7–10)

Come, my children, listen to me;
    I will teach you the fear of the LORD.
                         (PSALM 34:11)

Whoever of you loves life
    and desires to see many good days,
keep your tongue from evil
    and your lips from telling lies.
                         (PSALM 34:12–13)

The LORD makes firm the steps
    of the one who delights in him;
though he may stumble, he will not fall,
    for the LORD upholds him with his hand.
                         (PSALM 37:23–24)

"Love your enemies, do good to those who hate you,
bless those who curse you, pray for those who mistreat
you." (Luke 6:27–28 NASB)

The righteous cry out, and the LORD hears them;
    he delivers them from all their troubles.

(PSALM 34:17)

The LORD is close to the brokenhearted
    and saves those who are crushed in spirit.

(PSALM 34:18)

The righteous person may have many troubles,
    but the LORD delivers him from them all;
he protects all his bones,
    not one of them will be broken.

(PSALM 34:19–20)

Chapter 12: The Enemy's Plan Against You

Your enemy the devil prowls around like a roaring lion
looking for someone to devour. (1 Peter 5:8)

For everything in the world—the cravings of sinful man,
the lust of his eyes and the boasting of what he has and
does—comes not from the Father, but from the world.
(1 John 2:16)

Man does not live on bread alone but on every word that
comes from the mouth of the LORD. (Deuteronomy 8:3)

Fear the LORD your God, serve him only and take your oaths in his name. (Deuteronomy 6:13)

Worship Him, your True God, and serve Him. (Deuteronomy 6:13 THE VOICE)

Whom have I in heaven but you?
    And earth has nothing I desire besides you.
My flesh and my heart may fail,
    but God is the strength of my heart
    and my portion forever.

(PSALM 73:25–26)

Do not put the LORD your God to the test. (Deuteronomy 6:16)

Fear the LORD your God, serve him only and take your oaths in his name. Do not follow other gods, the gods of the peoples around you; for the LORD your God, who is among you, is a jealous God. (Deuteronomy 6:13–15)

Chapter 13: Miracles in the Mess

They laughed at him. (Mark 5:40)

They drove out many demons and anointed many sick people with oil and healed them. (Mark 6:13)

And they took offense at him. (Mark 6:3)

. . . because so many people were coming and going that they did not even have a chance to eat. (Mark 6:31)

Later that night, the boat was in the middle of the lake, and he was alone on land. He saw the disciples straining at the oars, because the wind was against them. (Mark 6:47–48)

They cried out, because they all saw him and were terrified.

Immediately he spoke to them and said, "Take courage! It is I. Don't be afraid." Then he climbed into the boat with them, and the wind died down. They were completely amazed, for they had not understood about the loaves; their hearts were hardened. (Mark 6:49–52)

. . . for they had not gained any insight from the incident of the loaves, but their heart was hardened. (Mark 6:52 NASB)

Do not conform to the pattern of this world, but be transformed by the renewing of your mind. (Romans 12:2)

God is our refuge and strength,
    an ever-present help in trouble.
Therefore we will not fear, though the earth give way
    and the mountains fall into the heart of the sea,
though its waters roar and foam
    and the mountains quake with their surging.

There is a river whose streams make glad the city of God,
    the holy place where the Most High dwells.

God is within her, she will not fall;
 God will help her at break of day.
Nations are in uproar, kingdoms fall;
 he lifts his voice, the earth melts.

The LORD Almighty is with us;
 the God of Jacob is our fortress.

Come and see what the LORD has done,
 the desolations he has brought on the earth.
He makes wars cease
 to the ends of the earth.
He breaks the bow and shatters the spear;
 he burns the shields with fire.
He says, "Be still, and know that I am God."

(PSALM 46:1–10)

Chapter 14: Moving Through the Desperate In-Between

Whoever dwells in the shelter of the Most High
 will rest in the shadow of the Almighty.
I will say of the LORD, "He is my refuge and my fortress,
 my God, in whom I trust."

Surely he will save you
 from the fowler's snare
 and from the deadly pestilence.
He will cover you with his feathers,
 and under his wings you will find refuge;

his faithfulness will be your shield and rampart.
You will not fear the terror of night,
    nor the arrow that flies by day,
nor the pestilence that stalks in the darkness,
    nor the plague that destroys at midday.
A thousand may fall at your side,
    ten thousand at your right hand,
    but it will not come near you.
You will only observe with your eyes
    and see the punishment of the wicked.

If you say, "The LORD is my refuge,"
    and you make the Most High your dwelling,
no harm will overtake you,
    no disaster will come near your tent.
For he will command his angels concerning you
    to guard you in all your ways;
they will lift you up in their hands,
    so that you will not strike your foot against a stone.
You will tread on the lion and the cobra;
    you will trample the great lion and the serpent.

"Because he loves me," says the LORD, "I will rescue him;
    I will protect him, for he acknowledges my name.
He will call on me, and I will answer him;
    I will be with him in trouble,
    I will deliver him and honor him.
With long life I will satisfy him
    and show him my salvation."

(PSALM 91)

Chapter 15: I Want to Run Away

"If you carefully observe all these commands I am giving
you to follow—to love the LORD your God, to walk in
obedience to him and to hold fast to him—then the
LORD will drive out all these nations before you, and you
will dispossess nations larger and stronger than you."
(Deuteronomy 11:22–23)

After saying these things, Jesus crossed the Kidron
Valley with his disciples and entered a grove of olive
trees. Judas, the betrayer, knew this place, because Jesus
had often gone there with his disciples. (John 18:1–2
NLT)

"My soul is overwhelmed with sorrow to the point of
death . . . Stay here and keep watch." (Mark 14:34)

Going a little farther, he fell to the ground and prayed
that if possible the hour might pass from him. "Abba,
Father," he said, "everything is possible for you. Take this
cup from me . . ." (Mark 14:35–36)

"Yet not what I will, but what you will." (Mark 14:36)

"I will lead the blind by ways they have not known,
along unfamiliar paths I will guide them; I will turn the
darkness into light before them and make the rough
places smooth. These are the things I will do; I will not
forsake them." (Isaiah 42:16)

We are . . . pressed . . . but not crushed. (2 Corinthians 4:8)

We are troubled on every side, yet not distressed; we are perplexed, but not in despair; persecuted, but not forsaken; cast down, but not destroyed. (2 Corinthians 4:8–9 KJV)

Bonus Chapter: What's It Like to Do Life with Me?

"Go now to your people in exile and speak to them. Say to them, 'This is what the Sovereign LORD says,' whether they listen or fail to listen." (Ezekiel 3:11)

My son, pay attention to what I say;
    turn your ear to my words.
Do not let them out of your sight,
    keep them within your heart;
for they are life to those who find them
    and health to one's whole body.

(PROVERBS 4:20–22)

Above all else, guard your heart,
    for everything you do flows from it.
Keep your mouth free of perversity;
    keep corrupt talk far from your lips.
Let your eyes look straight ahead;
    fix your gaze directly before you.
Give careful thought to the paths for your feet
    and be steadfast in all your ways.

Do not turn to the right or the left;
  keep your foot from evil.

(PROVERBS 4:23–27)

His pride led to his downfall. He was unfaithful to the
LORD his God. (2 Chronicles 26:16)

In his pride the wicked man does not seek him;
  in all his thoughts there is no room for God.

(PSALM 10:4)

For the sins of their mouths,
  for the words of their lips,
  let them be caught in their pride.

(PSALM 59:12)

When pride comes, then comes disgrace,
  but with humility comes wisdom.

(PROVERBS 11:2)

Where there is strife, there is pride,
  but wisdom is found in those who take advice.

(PROVERBS 13:10)

Pride goes before destruction,
  a haughty spirit before a fall.

(PROVERBS 16:18)

Things I Don't Want
You to Forget

$\backsim$

Chapter 1: I'd Rather Ignore Honesty

Honesty isn't trying to *hurt* me. It's trying to *heal* me.

Rejection steals the *best* of who I am by reinforcing the *worst* of what's been said to me.

If you want to know what's really inside a person, *listen* carefully to the *words* she speaks.

Rejection isn't just an *emotion* we feel. It's a *message* that's sent to the *core* of who we are, causing us to believe *lies* about ourselves, others, and God.

Chapter 2: Three Questions We Must Consider

When a man is physically *present* but emotionally *absent*, a girl's heart can feel quite *hollow* and *helpless*.

The mind *feasts* on what it *focuses* on. What consumes my thinking will be the *making* or the *breaking* of my identity.

The beliefs we hold should hold us up even when life *feels* like it's *falling* apart.

God is *good*. God is good to me. God is good at being God.

No person's rejection can ever exempt me from God's love for me. *Period*. No question mark.

Chapter 3: There's a Lady at the Gym Who Hates Me

Live from the *abundant* place that you are *loved*, and you won't find yourself *begging* others for *scraps* of love.

We run at a breakneck pace to try and *achieve* what God simply wants us to slow down enough to *receive*.

God wants our hearts to be in alignment *with* Him before our hands set about doing today's assignment *for* Him.

God's love isn't *based* on me. It's simply *placed* on me. And it's the place from which I should live . . . loved.

Giving with strings of secret *expectations* attached is the greatest invitation to *heartbreak*.

Jesus doesn't participate in the rat race. He's into the slower rhythms of life, like *abiding*, *delighting*, and *dwelling*—all words that require us to trust Him with our place and our pace.

How *dangerous* it is when our souls are *gasping* for God but we're too distracted *flirting* with the world to notice.

Chapter 4: Alone in a Crowded Room

Proximity and *activity* don't always equal *connectivity*.

The *more* we *fill* ourselves from His life-giving *love*, the *less* we will be *dictated* by the grabby-ness of the *flesh*.

The more fully we *invite* God in, the less we will feel *uninvited* by others.

Chapter 5: Hello, My Name Is Trust Issues

What we see will *violate* what we *know* unless what we know dictates what we *see*.

With the fullness of God, we are *free* to let humans be humans—*fickle* and *fragile* and *forgetful*.

If we become *enamored* with something in this world we think offers better *fullness* than God, we will make room for it. We leak out His fullness to make room for something else we want to *chase*.

Chapter 6: Friendship Breakups

People who care more about *being* right than *ending* *right* prove just how *wrong* they were all along.

Bitterness, resentment, and *anger* have no place in a *heart* as *beautiful* as yours.

We have an *enemy*, and it's not each other.

Truth proclaimed and lived out is a *fiercely* accurate weapon against *evil*.

Chapter 7: When Our Normal Gets Snatched

I can't continue to fully *embrace* God while *rejecting* His ways.

Grace given when it feels least deserved is the only antidote for *bitter* rot.

To *love* God is to *cooperate* with His grace.

Each hole left from rejection must become an *opportunity* to create more and more space for *grace* in my heart.

Humility can't be bought at a *bargain* price. It's the long *working* of grace upon grace within the *hurts* of our hearts.

It's *impossible* to hold up the banners of *victim* and *victory* at the same time.

Chapter 8: The Corrective Experience

Relationships don't come in packages of *perfection*; relationships come in packages of *potential*.

"Me too" puts us on the same *team*. It says, "We are in this *together*, so let's *attack* the *problem*, not each other."

Acceptance is like an *antibiotic* that prevents past *rejections* from turning into present-day *infections*.

No amount of *outside* achievement fixes *inside* hurts.

Chapter 9: Why Does Rejection Hurt So Much?

To be set *aside* is to be rejected. To be set *apart* is to be given an assignment that requires preparation.

The *tweaking* of us by God in the *quiet* is the *saving* of us in *public*.

There is something wonderfully *sacred* that happens when a girl chooses to realize that being set aside is actually God's *call* for her to be set apart.

When I ease the *loneliness* ache in others, it is beautifully eased in me.

Chapter 10: Her Success Does Not Threaten Mine

If we allow our thoughts to *stink*, that smell will *leak* out of every bit of us—our words, our actions, and especially our reactions.

There is an *abundant* need in this world for your exact brand of *beautiful*.

As Jesus girls, we can't walk in *victory* while wallowing in thoughts of *defeat* and rejection.

When she does well, we all do well. All tides *rise* when we see a sister making this world a *better* place with her *gifts*.

Chapter 11: Ten Things You Must Remember When Rejected

Today's *disappointment* is making room for tomorrow's *appointment*.

Don't let today's *reaction* become tomorrow's *regret*.

God isn't *afraid* of your *sharp* edges that may seem quite *risky* to others. He doesn't pull back. He pulls you *close*.

Satan knows what *consumes* us *controls* us.

There is usually some element of *protection* wrapped in every *rejection*.

There's much *more* to you than the part that was rejected.

This *breaking* of you will be the *making* of you. A new you. A *stronger* you.

Chapter 12: The Enemy's Plan Against You

Lies flee in the presence of *truth*.

The Devil is *vicious*, but he's not *victorious*. And you, my friend, have everything you need to *defeat* him.

When I remember the *promises* of God,
I tap into the *power* of God.

Our *minds* and *hearts* are like dry sponges. What we
focus on is what will *soak* in and *saturate* us.

Is my attention being held by something *sacred*
or something *secret?* What is holding my attention the
most is what I'm *truly* worshipping.

Chapter 13: Miracles in the Mess

Inspiration and *information* without personal *application* will never amount to *transformation*.

Resisting God's promises will make us *forget* God's presence.

The voices of *condemnation, shame,*
and *rejection* can come at you, but they don't
have to reside in you.

We can go to Bible study and *amen* every point made, but if we don't *apply* it to our lives, we won't be changed.

He's not running from your *mess*. He's *climbing* in it to be right there with you.

Chapter 14: Moving Through the Desperate In-Between

We must *feel* the pain to *heal* the pain.

Fear can't *catch* what it can no longer *reach*.

Pain is the *invitation* for God to move in and replace our *faltering* strength with His.

Numbing the pain never goes to the source of the real issue to make us healthier. It only *silences* our screaming need for help.

If we *avoid* the hurt, the hurt creates a *void* in us.

Chapter 15: I Want to Run Away

Heartbreaking seasons can certainly *grow* me but were never meant to *define* me.

On the other side of every hardship is a *resurrection*.

People can't *fix* from the outside a *perspective* that needs to be *rewired* on the inside. Only the Lord can do that.

Chapter 16: What I Thought Would Fix Me Didn't

The *spotlight* never fixes our insecurities. It only *magnifies* what we thought popularity would *cover* up.

Rejection may be a delay or *distraction* or even a *devastation* for a season. But it's never a final *destination*.

It's not about you *becoming* anything. Your soul was made to simply *be* with Me. And the more you are with Me, the more you will stop *fearing* what the world might take from you.

With You, Jesus, I'm forever *safe*. I'm forever *accepted*. I'm forever *held*. Completely *loved* and always *invited* in.

Bonus Chapter: What's It Like to Do Life with Me?

The *less* we feel we need to address *pride* in our lives, the more it has already *blinded* us.

Wisdom seeks to see someone else's vantage point even if I don't agree with that person's *perspective*.

Notes

Chapter 2: Three Questions We Must Consider

1. "C. S. Lewis Quotes, Quotable Quotes," Good Reads, accessed February 22, 2016, http://www.goodreads.com /quotes/615-we-are-not-necessarily-doubting-that-god-will-do-the.

Chapter 8: The Corrective Experience

1. Aaron Ben-Zeév PhD, "Why We All Need to Belong to Someone," *PsychologyToday.com*, March 11, 2014, https:// www.psychologytoday.com/blog/in-the-name-love/201403 /why-we-all-need-belong-someone.

2. Read 1 Samuel 16:1–13 for the full story.

Chapter 9: Why Does Rejection Hurt So Much?

1. Guy Winch, PhD, "10 Surprising Facts About Rejection," *PsychologyToday.com*, July 3, 2013, https://www .psychologytoday.com/blog/the-squeaky-wheel/201307/10-surprising-facts-about-rejection.

2. John 3:29–30 (THE MESSAGE).

Chapter 10: Her Success Does Not Threaten Mine

1. http://biblehub.com/commentaries/ellicott/2_corinthians/2.htm.

2. Stephen R. Covey, *The 7 Habits of Highly Effective People: Powerful Lessons in Personal Change* (New York: Simon and Schuster, 2004), 219.

3. Walter Brueggermann, "The Liturgy of Abundance, The Myth of Scarcity," *Christian Century,* March 24–31, l999. Walter Brueggermann is professor emeritus of Old Testament at Columbia Theological Seminary in Decatur, Georgia. Copyright by the Christian Century Foundation and used by permission. This text was prepared for Religion Online by John C. Purdy.

Chapter 12: The Enemy's Plan Against You

1. The Barna research study included 455 surveys among a representative, random sample of women ages 18 and older in the United States. The survey, conducted between April 29 through May 1, 2015, utilized the web-enabled KnowledgePanel which is based on probability sampling that covers both the online and offline populations in the U.S. The estimated maximum sampling error for the aggregate sample is plus or minus 4.5 percent at the 95 percent confidence level.

Chapter 15: I Want to Run Away

1. Add a visual dynamic to what you're reading here about the olive tree with the *Uninvited Bible Study* DVD.

Bonus Chapter

1. Robert L. Alden, *Proverbs: A Commentary on an Ancient Book of Timeless Advice* (Grand Rapids: Baker, 1983), 48.

About the Author

Photo by The Schultzes

Lysa TerKeurst is a wife to Art and mom to five priority blessings named Jackson, Mark, Hope, Ashley, and Brooke. She is the president of Proverbs 31 Ministries and author of nineteen books, including the *New York Times* bestsellers *The Best Yes, Unglued,* and *Made to Crave.* Additionally, Lysa has been featured on *Focus on the Family, The Today Show, Good Morning America,* and more. Lysa speaks nationwide at Catalyst, Lifeway Abundance Conference, Women of Joy, and various church events.

To those who know her best, Lysa is simply a woman who loves Jesus passionately, is dedicated to her family, and struggles like the rest of us with laundry, junk drawers, and cellulite.

Website: If you enjoyed *Uninvited*, equip yourself with additional resources at www.UninvitedBook.com, www.LysaTerKeurst.com, and www.Proverbs31.org.

Connect with Lysa on a daily basis, see pictures of her family, and follow her speaking schedule:
Blog: www.LysaTerKeurst.com
Facebook: www.Facebook.com/OfficialLysa
Instagram: @LysaTerKeurst
Twitter: @LysaTerKeurst

About Proverbs 31 Ministries

Lysa TerKeurst is the president of Proverbs 31 Ministries, located in Charlotte, North Carolina.

If you were inspired by *Uninvited* and desire to deepen your own personal relationship with Jesus Christ, we have just what you're looking for.

Proverbs 31 Ministries exists to be a trusted friend who will take you by the hand and walk by your side, leading you one step closer to the heart of God through:

Free *First 5* app
Free online daily devotions
Online Bible studies
Writer and speaker training
Daily radio programs
Books and resources

For more information about Proverbs 31 Ministries, visit
www.Proverbs31.org.

To inquire about having Lysa speak at your event, visit
www.LysaTerKeurst.com and click on "speaking."

Free gifts for you!

You know those desperate moments where life's hurts and rejections make you feel helpless?

Infuse God's hope and power into your heart with Lysa's FREE audio recording of "Prayers to Press Through Rejection." Based on Psalm 91, these deeply personal and healing prayers will help you declare God's promises over your life.

Visit www.proverbs31.org /uninvitedgift to download yours.

Stop allowing rejection to steal the best of who you are with help from the declarations found in "10 Things You Must Remember When Rejected."

Visit www.proverbs31.org /uninvitedgift to download your FREE printable copy today.

Uninvited DVD and Study Guide

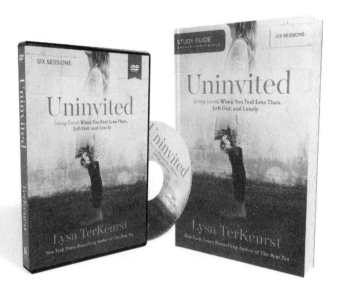

A ll of us are either healing from a past rejection, dealing with a present rejection, or fearing an unexpected rejection could be coming our way. Join Lysa in this six-session video Bible study as she digs deep into God's Word to help women explore the roots of rejection, the way other relationships get tainted because of a past rejection, and the truth about what it looks like to live loved. Filmed in the Holy Land, each session takes participants on a visual journey to some of the places where people such as Hannah, David, and even Jesus Himself lived and walked. The corresponding study guide is packed full of deep Bible teaching, guided group study questions, and personal reflection as well as in-between-sessions study material.

ALSO AVAILABLE
FROM LYSA

Are you living with the stress of an overwhelmed schedule and aching with the sadness of an underwhelmed soul?

www.TheBestYes.com

CURRICULUM
ALSO
AVAILABLE!